DENISE AFFONÇO
Cambodia. Her m
When the Maoist Khmer Rouge seized power in April 1975, her peaceful life was torn apart. She was deported with her husband, a communist idealist, and their two children to the countryside, where her husband was taken away by the Khmer Rouge and never seen again. Her daughter died of starvation. In 1979, four hellish years were brought to an end when the Vietnamese invaded. Today, Denise is remarried, lives in Paris and works at the EU's Institute for Security Studies.

DAVID CHANDLER is an emeritus professor of history at Monash University in Melbourne, Australia. He is the author of seven books on Cambodian history and politics which include: *A History of Cambodia (4th edition 2007), Facing the Cambodian Past: Selected Essays (1995)* and *Voices from S-21: Terror and History in Pol Pot's Secret Prison (1999).*

JON SWAIN is an award-winning British *Sunday Times* Senior Foreign Correspondent, who caught the last commercial flight into Cambodia in 1975. It was there that he witnessed the fall of the city to the Khmer Rouge. He covered the war in IndoChina between 1975 and 1979 and has returned numerous times to report from Cambodia. He is the author of *River of Time: A Memoir of Vietnam and Cambodia (1995)* . His experience was immortalised in the critically acclaimed film, *The Killing Fields (1984).*

Denise Affonço

TO THE END OF HELL

One Woman's Struggle to Survive Cambodia's Khmer Rouge

Translated from the French by Margaret Burn *and* Katie Hogben

With introductions by David Chandler *and* Jon Swain

rp

REPORTAGE PRESS

REPORTAGE PRESS

Published by Reportage Press
26 Richmond Way, London W12 8LY, United Kingdom
Tel: +44-7971-461-935 Fax: +44-208-749-2867
e-mail: info@reportagepress.com
www.reportagepress.com

To the End of Hell was produced under the editorial direction
of Laura Keeling

First published in France as
'*La digue des veuves – rescapée de l'enfer des Khmers rouges.*'
by Presses de la Renaissance in 2005

First published in Great Britain in 2007 by Reportage Press
Second edition published in Great Britain in 2008 by Reportage Press

British Library Cataloguing in Publication Data.
A catalogue record for this book is available from the British Library.
ISBN-13: 978-1-906702-07-6

Cover design by Joshua Haymann and layout by Marine Galtier

Printed and bound in Great Britain by
CPI Bookmarque, Croydon, CR0 4TD
www.antonyrowe.co.uk

For my daughter Jeannie

Acknowledgements

My particular thanks are due to David Chandler to whom I am profoundly grateful for his encouragement. I would also like to thank my friend Colette Ledannois, without whom this book would never have seen the light of day, Martine Legrand, Cécile Benoliel, Valéry Giscard d'Estaing, Michel Deverge and his kind friends and, of course, my French family.

Introduction *by Jon Swain*

The Killing Fields of Cambodia are a thing of the past. Pol Pot, whose drive to create an agrarian utopia killed millions and turned it into a madhouse, is dead. The country today is an important stop on the Southeast Asian tourist trail and no longer seemingly eternally at war with itself.

But Cambodia is a place that takes over the soul. The memories fade slowly. Those who knew it at its worst during the years of war and the Khmer Rouge tyranny more than a quarter of a century ago are irresistibly drawn back to confront their physical and emotional wounds.

Long after the soldiers have gone, the legacy of war remains: in the cripples on crutches living on handouts, in the landmines, in the pain of memory and in the shrines of skulls to those murdered by the Khmer Rouge. Not even the sheer heavenly beauty of the fabled temples of Angkor, the golden age of the Khmer empire that once dominated much of Indochina, will erase them.

Since 1975, I have been back many times and met many Cambodian survivors. None of them have been able to bury the horrors they endured. Some have recorded their experiences in memoirs. Denise Affonço has written one of the most memorable of them. Up to two million people were executed or died from disease and starvation during the Pol Pot years, nearly a third of the population, and her book *To the End of Hell* speaks for all Cambodians who suffered and perished under the Khmer Rouge.

Today, Denise lives in a neat world in France where people weep over a single death, do not hear gunfire and almost nothing happens to disturb the peaceful flow of their lives. But on April 17, 1975, this Frenchwoman – daughter of a French father of Indian heritage and a Vietnamese mother – who had a job in the cultural section of the French embassy in Phnom Penh, found herself trapped in the besieged Cambodian capital with her children and their father, Seng, a Cambodian of Chinese origin.

Against her better judgement, Denise had decided to stay behind as the Khmer Rouge victory approached. As French citizens, she and her children had the right to be repatriated to the safety of France. The French embassy was ready to evacuate them. But it was more complicated for Seng, a non-Frenchman, so, rather than split up the family, which she thought would be wrong, she elected that they should all stay together.

Also Seng, a naive, armchair communist who was looking forward to the victory of the Khmer Rouge, convinced her that staying behind would be safe. She soon found how tragically wrong he would be.

As I read her book, I too can see scarred and war-battered Phnom Penh again. The city had somehow managed to retain something of the air of a French provincial town for much of the war. But now, as the conflict moved towards its horrifying end, life was collapsing. Thousands were starving or living on handouts and the hospitals were heaving with untreated wounded.

As the Khmer Rouge closed in there was fear and panic in the streets. The Americans had closed down their embassy and evacuated their staff in a helicopter-borne operation a few days before, bringing an end to their violent, destructive involvement in a once-gentle land that they had pounded with B-52 strikes. Now the people of the city waited in a mixture of fear and hope for the Khmer Rouge to arrive.

Who knows, I might have walked or driven passed Denise in those last days when I was also in beleaguered Phnom Penh. The hotel where I and other journalists covering the war lived was only a few hundred yards down the Boulevard Monivong from the French embassy where she was working. Her children went to school at the Lycée Descartes just across the road from the hotel.

That was Denise's life until the fateful day when the Khmer Rouge marched in. They arrived with Maoist hats, rifles and eyes as cold and sharp as stone. Immediately after taking the city they started to empty it of its population at gunpoint.

As one of the few western journalists to have remained behind to witness the fall of the city, I was sheltering inside the French embassy with other foreigners who had been ordered to regroup there by the Khmer Rouge authorities.

We were defenceless and became virtual prisoners. A handful of unarmed gendarmes manned the gate. The Khmer Rouge did not recognise the embassy as French territory and could shoot their way in at any time. They stayed outside but forced the French to expel all the Cambodians seeking refuge with them.

The people of Phnom Penh were streaming past the embassy gates in their thousands – the old, the sick, the hungry, the orphans and little children. Even the twenty thousand wounded in the hospitals hobbled by, bandaged and trying to hold each other up or being wheeled down the road in their hospital beds, serum and plasma bottles still attached.

We did not fully realise it at the time, but we were witnessing the start of one of the world's most terrifying attempts to create an agrarian communist utopia. The Khmer Rouge turned Cambodia back to Year Zero.

Denise and her family joined the exodus out of the city on this forced trek into an unknown hell. They did not pass the embassy, leaving by another road. But the terror was the same whichever route out of Phnom Penh people took. From that moment on life for her, and for all who were dear to her, became a struggle for survival.

Had she sheltered in the French embassy, she and her children might have escaped to France when we westerners were evacuated overland to Thailand some weeks later. So, too, perhaps would have Seng. But it was not to be.

During the next three years, eight months and twenty-one days, until they were overthrown, the Khmer Rouge held Cambodia in a paralysing grip. To our eternal anguish, many of our Cambodian and Asian friends who had taken shelter in the embassy were forced to leave under Khmer Rouge threats. The French saw no other choice but to order them out after the Khmer Rouge threatened to invade the embassy and take the Cambodians out at gunpoint. Almost all who were forced out were executed in cruel and obscure ways; others died of starvation. I still remember the anguish of Jean Dyrac, the French consul, on whose shoulders fell this terrible decision. "We are no longer men", he said.

Like all the evacuees, Denise and her family thought the evacuation was temporary and they would soon be allowed to return to Phnom Penh. It never happened. They became part of a dehumanised labour force toiling long hours in the fields. She knew starvation, disease and violence. She had hunger stamped on her face, but the endlessness of the nightmare never quite crushed her will to survive even after she had lost Seng, the father of her children, and her beloved daughter Jeannie.

Seng was summoned one day into the forest by Angkar Leu, the Khmer Rouge organisation on high, and executed like other intellectuals, professionals and especially soldiers who had been associated with the former regime. Misery piled on misery. Aged nine, Jeannie faded away and died. This book is dedicated to her.

In January 1979 the Vietnamese invaded Cambodia and chased the Khmer Rouge from power. The fighting enabled Denise to run away and, hollow-cheeked and desperately ill, she was saved by a kindly Vietnamese army doctor who nursed her back to health. Eventually she was able to make her way to France, where she lives today.

Denise's book is an extension of an account of her suffering which she first wrote in the immediate aftermath at the request of the Vietnamese authorities, who wanted to use it as evidence in a war crimes trial of the Khmer Rouge leadership, which they were holding in Phnom Penh of the Khmer Rouge leadership. That court received no international legitimacy. Shunning the new government that the Vietnamese communists had set up to replace the Khmer Rouge as a puppet regime, the West ignored it, considering it a political showcase trial.

The truth is, as Denise acknowledges, that Vietnamese military intervention saved the lives of countless Cambodians who were condemned to die. They included Denise and the rest of her family, who were by then at death's door and who owe the Vietnamese their lives.

But the West, particularly America, was suspicious and unsympathetic towards Vietnamese intentions. At the time, the Cold War was in full swing and Vietnam was firmly in the Soviet camp. The West saw Vietnam's intervention as evidence of its desire to dominate the whole of IndoChina. The fact is that the evidence of Khmer Rouge crimes that was laid before the court cannot be disputed. In fact, the passing of time has brought to light even more horrors.

In 2005, when Denise's book was published in Britain, agreement was finally reached between the United Nations and the Cambodian government of Prime Minister Hung Seng, after years of stalling and bickering, to bring the surviving Khmer Rouge leaders responsible on trial.

The UN sponsored court is too late for Pol Pot. He died in the jungle in 1998 in a zone of Cambodia still controlled by his Khmer Rouge guerrillas. But several top leaders of the genocide survived him and are still alive to face trial.

One of those due to go on trial is Comrade Duch, the regime's chief torturer during the period of the 'killing fields', who had run the Toul Sleng Lycée in Phnom Penh as an extermination camp. Under his direction the Lycée became a portal of death for thousands. While Khmer Rouge records show twenty thousand were murdered there, many are missing and Duch has acknowledged responsibility for forty thousand deaths.

Many victims were members of the Khmer Rouge itself, re-labelled traitors in Duch's paranoid world as the regime devoured itself. Confessions were extracted using whips, chains, water baths and poisonous reptiles. In one case he ordered the purging of an entire Khmer Rouge battalion, including two nine-year-old soldiers, because it was thought disloyal. "Kill them all", he wrote.

Survivors will always wonder how it is that the hour of retribution has taken so long to come for such murderers. Denise's scars will always be there. There is not a single thing that can compensate for the death of her daughter Jeannie and the deaths of nearly two million people. Her journey from war-torn Cambodia through its killing fields to France is an extraordinary, often painful, but poignantly uplifting odyssey. The tearful goodbyes she said to her beloved daughter as she lay, hollow-cheeked and skin and bone, and died is long in the past.

But she would still like to hear from their mouths why it happened.

Jon Swain, London 2007

Preface *by David Chandler*

On 17 April 1975, thousands of Cambodian Khmer Rouge insurgents marched into Phnom Penh and ended the five-year war they had waged, often with Vietnamese assistance, against the ill-fated, corrupt and pro-American Khmer Republic. Over the next few days, everyone in the city – including the author of this absorbing memoir – was expelled into the countryside. They were told over loudspeakers to take up rural occupations. In the exodus, thousands of them died and thousands of others were separated from their families.

From then on, life for nearly everyone in Cambodia went from bad to worse. The entire nation was subjected to the swiftest and most radical Marxist-Leninist revolution in world history. Leaders of the Khmer Rouge, many of whom had been partly educated in France, boasted that there were no precedents for what they were doing. Calling themselves 'the revolutionary organisation' (*angkar pakdevat*) they abolished money, religious practices, markets, urban life and formal education. They forced everyone to wear peasant costumes and forbade them from speaking any languages but Khmer. As the brutal, utopian and anonymous regime tore Cambodia apart, nearly two million people died of starvation, overwork, misdiagnosed diseases and executions.

People who survived the Khmer Rouge years have written numerous memoirs, but Denise Affonço's testimony is of peculiar interest and has a special value. Its virtues spring from the uniqueness of Denise Affonço's life history (and thus from her unique vantage-point), from the almost mythic trajectory of her life between 1975 and 1980 and from the skill and clarity with which she has set down her experiences under the Khmer Rouge and under the first eleven months of the Vietnamese protectorate that followed.

Denise Affonço was a child of the French Empire. Her father was an Indian-Portuguese French citizen from Pondicherry, the French colonial outpost in India, her mother was a Vietnamese, domiciled in Cambodia. Raised by her parents in Phnom Penh, where her father was an official in the colonial school system, young Denise attended French schools. For this reason, she seldom spoke the Cambodian language, and never learned to read it. Instead, she thought of herself, and thinks of herself today, "in her soul" as French. Throughout her ordeal under the Khmer Rouge she always hoped to be repatriated to France, *la mère patrie* (which she had never seen). Her hope sustained her through horrific times. Her repatriation at the end of 1979 gives her memoir its unexpectedly happy ending.

Denise attended the Francophone Lycée Descartes in Phnom Penh. Soon after graduating she started work at the French Embassy. At about the same time, she met her partner, a handsome Chinese entrepreneur named Phou Teang Seng. The couple had three children, one of whom died in infancy. Seng was a talented engineer, a *bon vivant* and an armchair Communist. He enjoyed praising the achievements of the Chinese revolution and deriding those of France, but he also enjoyed his comforts and his wealth. He and his wife argued about politics, but they were fond of each other and devoted to their children.

Everything changed after April 17, when the couple and their extended family, nine people in all, set out into exile in Seng's Chevrolet. The Khmer Rouge in the countryside south of Phnom Penh expropriated the car, and the family lingered and worked as farmers in the region for five months. In July 1975, Seng disappeared. He was undoubtedly executed, probably for his entrepreneurial past and his misplaced bonhomie, which the dour Khmer Rouge cadre interpreted as treason.

Two months later, the young widow and her two children were evacuated with hundreds of others to Phnom Leap in north-western Cambodia. Their experiences there over the next two years and three months form the core of the memoir. As so-called 'new people' (i.e. those who had never supported the revolution, and had lived in cities during the civil war) they were harshly treated, and told that their lives were not worth a bullet to kill them with. To keep you is no gain, they were told. "To destroy you is no loss."

The work was gruelling. There was never enough for anyone to eat. Denise Affonço's nine-year-old daughter, Jeannie, died of starvation in November 1976. So did hundreds of others at the work site. Over the next two years, Denise soldiered on, silent and enraged, keeping track of her young son. They both survived.

The regime collapsed following the Vietnamese invasion in January 1979. The pages that describe the next eleven months are of interest, because Denise Affonço's fluency in Vietnamese allowed her to obtain useful work almost at once — first in a hospital in Siem Reap and later with the newly re-established Ministry of Health in Phnom Penh. She was also encouraged by the Vietnamese to write her memoirs of the Khmer Rouge period. In August 1979, Denise was an eloquent witness at the show trial, staged by the Vietnamese, of the Khmer Rouge leaders Pol Pot and Ieng Sary, who were both condemned to death in absentia.

Despite Vietnamese kindness and steady, rewarding work, Denise Affonço had no rationale for staying in Cambodia. Throughout 1979, she pressured anyone with contacts outside the country to consider her case as a French citizen seeking to be repatriated to France. She eventually won the battle and the main body of the book ends with her departure, with her son, from Ho Chi Minh City en route to Paris.

It is an honour and a privilege for me to introduce this powerful and moving book to a wide audience of readers. Some years ago, in the course of my research, I met Denise Affonço in Paris, and interviewed her about her experiences under the Khmer Rouge. What she told me then was useful for a book that I was writing about Cambodia's recent past.

These far more extended memories, written in an elegant, accessible style, bear eloquent witness not only to a horrible period of Cambodian history and the almost unbearable sufferings of the author, but also to the steadfastness and integrity of a brave survivor.

David Chandler
Monash University, Melbourne

Chronology

1863   Cambodia becomes a French protectorate. French colonial rule lasts for ninety years.

1953   Cambodia wins its independence from France and becomes the Kingdom of Cambodia.

1965   King Sihanouk breaks off relations with the United States. He allows North Vietnamese guerrillas to set up bases in Cambodia in order to pursue their campaign against the US-backed government in South Vietnam.

1969   The US begins a secret bombing campaign against North Vietnamese forces on Cambodian soil.

1970   18 March: Supported by the US, General Lon Nol seizes power in a coup d'état. King Norodom Sihanouk is stripped of his role as head of state. The Republic of Cambodia is proclaimed. Lon Nol sends an army to fight the North Vietnamese in Cambodia. Sihanouk, now in exile in China, forms a guerrilla movement as do the Khmer Rouge.

April: Vietnamese in Phnom Penh are rounded up

and sent to concentration camps.

1971   Pogroms begin against Vietnamese residents suspected of harbouring communist Vietnamese soldiers, especially in the Kompong Speu and Kompong Thom provinces. The massacres are led by Lon Nol's government troops.

1975   17 April: Lon Nol is overthrown by the Khmer Rouge, which is led by Pol Pot and Ieng Sary. The Khmer Rouge enter Phnom Penh in triumph. Proclamation of the state of Democratic Kampuchea.

18 April: A mass exodus begins as the population of Phnom Penh are forcibly driven out of the capital. 'Year Zero' is declared. Money, private property, education and religion are all abolished. Hundreds of thousands of the educated middle-classes are tortured and executed in special centres. Others starve, or die from disease or exhaustion. The total death toll during the next three years is unknown. Estimates range from 1.7 million (twenty-one per cent of the population) to 3 million. Given that Cambodia had a population of just seven million when the Khmer Rouge seized power, the genocide is proportionally one of the world's worst.

Sept. 1975 – Jan. 1979 A second deportation occurs. Hundreds of thousands of refugees are forced to leave the east and the south for the north-west of the country.

1977   Fighting breaks out with Vietnam.

1978   Vietnamese forces invade Cambodia.

1979   January: The Khmer Rouge regime is overthrown by the Vietnamese.

1979-89 Establishment of the People's Republic of Kampuchea. The new state is not recognised by the international community. Pol Pot and the Khmer Rouge flee to the region near the border with Thailand. Cambodia is plagued by guerrilla warfare. Hundreds of thousands become refugees.

1989 Vietnamese troops withdraw. The Prime Minister Hun Sen abandons socialism in an attempt to attract foreign investment. The country is renamed the State of Cambodia. Buddhism is re-established as the state religion.

1991 King Sihanouk becomes head of state under a UN-brokered deal after thirteen years in exile.

1998 Former dictator Pol Pot dies in his jungle hideout.

2001 Senate approves a law to create a tribunal to bring genocide charges against Khmer Rouge leaders.

2005 April: A tribunal to try surviving Khmer Rouge leaders gets a green light from UN after years of debate about funding.

2004 Sihanouk resigns. Parliament ratifies a plan to establish a tribunal to try the Khmer Rouge leadership.

2007 Kaing Guek Eav, known as 'Comrade Duch', becomes the first surviving Khmer Rouge leader to be charged by the UN-backed tribunal. The first school textbook is produced covering the 1975-79 period of Khmer Rouge rule.

Denise Affonço's Cambodia

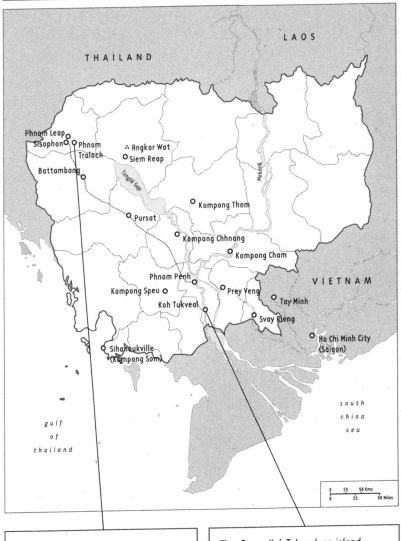

Second Camp: *The hamlet of Loti-Batran, close to Phnom Traloch. A mountainous, malarial region with virgin forests and marshes.*

First Camp: *Koh Tukveal, an island situated some sixty kilometres south of Phnom Penh.*

Foreword

On 7 January 1979, the Vietnamese Army enter Phnom Penh and liberate Cambodia from the yoke of the Khmer Rouge; the country emerges from four years of horror.

Towards the end of the same month I manage, with the help of my young son, to flee the jungle where the rest of my family and more than two million Cambodians have perished. I'm in a terrible state, emaciated and more dead than alive. For four years, I have lived off cockroaches, toads, rats, scorpions, grasshoppers and termites. For four years, I have been starved by the Khmer Rouge's brutal regime. Whatever the weather, I worked barefoot in muddy paddy fields – sowing, planting, reaping, digging ditches or building dykes. All I had ever eaten for breakfast was a few grains of rock salt and cold water. My body was swollen with famine, I was feverish with malaria and I was absolutely forbidden to mourn or cry for my dead.

Free at last, I manage to drag my thirty-kilo body to the nearest village where some Vietnamese soldiers, who are liberating the area, take us as far as Siem Reap, a province in the north-west of Cambodia. The refugees in this region are being cared for in a makeshift hospital. There a Vietnamese medical officer asks me to write an account of everything that I've seen and endured; later this will be used as evidence in the trial organised by the pro-Vietnamese Khmer government to try Pol Pot and his henchmen in absentia.

As soon as I am more or less recovered, I begin as quickly as I can to look for a way to leave this place that has been cursed by such a monstrous crime and to seek refuge in France, my father's country.

From 1980 onwards, I wasn't able to go back over my testimony of those four years of hard labour, as I was frightened of reprisals and far too busy, since I had had to start again from scratch once I had arrived in France. Then one day at work, I met a European academic. We started talking about genocide around the world I brought up the case of Cambodia. But the eminent professor interrupted me aggressively and said dryly that there had never been a problem in Cambodia: "I really don't understand why people always talk of a Khmer genocide. The Khmer Rouge only did good things for their country. I visited Phnom Penh in 1978 and everything was normal, the Cambodians were living happily and in perfect health." I was completely outraged by these remarks and replied curtly: "Professor, I was also there, not just in 1978, but from April 1975 to January 1979, not in Phnom Penh but in the forests where we were deported and treated like animals! The Khmer Rouge ignored the fact that I was a French citizen and sent me into forced labour; I was trapped in hell for four years!" The man's jaw dropped and he didn't say another word.

How could an intelligent man in such a position have allowed himself to have been so manipulated? After this incident, I realised that I absolutely had to pluck up the courage to set down in black and white the slow descent into hell that we were subjected to for four years. I had to do this in order to fight the thesis of denial of those intellectuals who never miss an opportunity to claim that the Khmer Rouge's reign of terror never happened, so that this macabre episode in Cambodia's history is not forgotten.

So I read over the notes that I had written while I was in a state of shock in Siem Reap. I delved painfully into the memories of a nightmarish past and put them in some kind of order ...

I dedicate this work to my little nine-year-old daughter who died of hunger and to all the loved ones lost or buried "somewhere, over there, in the depths of an inhospitable jungle".

TO THE END OF HELL

1/ Youth: The Good Life

I'm a pure product of colonialism – a Eurasian, born in Phnom Penh in November 1944, to a French father and a Vietnamese mother.

My father, Maurice Lucien Affonço, first saw the light of day in Pondicherry, then a French colony, which explains his nationality. But his origins were very mixed and, if a Portuguese ancestor gave him his name, it was without doubt a Hindu forebear who gave him his chocolate brown skin. From his first marriage to a girl from Alsace, who died of amoebic dysentery in 1931, he had three children; two boys, Henri and Bernard, whom he sent to France for their higher education, and a girl, Lydie, who studied at the French Lycée in Dalat, in Vietnam.

My father was recruited by the Ministry of Culture and arrived in Cambodia in 1921, to take up his post as head of the Ecole de Marbre in Pursat. In March 1945, during the Japanese occupation, he was rounded up along with all the other French and sent to a concentration camp. At the end of the war, he settled down in the country and was hired by the French Ministry of Education to teach French, English and Latin at the main Cambodian Lycée, Sisowath, in Phnom Penh. It was here, earlier, that he had met my mother, who came from the large Vietnamese community.

My father was also the private tutor of Prince Norodom

Sihanouk, who showed him both respect and friendship[1] . On important occasions, I remember that the King used to send one of his daughters to deliver baskets of rare fruit to us from abroad: apples, pears, peaches, cherries and apricots. When I arrived in France I was happy to rediscover the flavour of the fruit of *Samdech Euv*.[2]

My father was very strict with his daughters. I got the biggest slap of my life when I came home from school without having been enrolled on the honours board in my monthly school report! My sister Lydie told me that when she was at school and he had been her Latin teacher he had made her recite her lessons in front of the whole class, urged on by the swish of his cane. There's no denying that he didn't leave us with only happy memories.

Despite his mixed blood, his behaviour was sometimes quite racist. Take the time my sister got engaged to her gym teacher, who was from the West Indies … what hadn't she done wrong? The day this cultured and extremely nice young man came to Phnom Penh to get to know 'Mr. Affonço', my father made it quite clear that he would have preferred to see his daughter marry a white man. My sister retorted indignantly: "Listen, Papa, how long has it been since you last looked in the mirror?" As far as he was concerned that was an insult. From that day onwards, my brother-in-law never called his father-in-law anything other than 'Mr. Affonço'.

When my father retired, he decided to leave Cambodia and to join his eldest sons in France. Above all, he was very proud of his first blonde and blue-eyed grandson and wanted to get to know him. My mother couldn't go with him as she

---

1. The prince became king in 1941 at the age of nineteen.
2. In Cambodian *Samdech* means 'lord', 'prince' or 'excellency'; the Khmer people called Sihanouk "*Samdech Euv*" which means, literally, "Prince Dad".

had too many members of her own family to care for and, as I was still very young, my father did not want to separate me from her. So he left Cambodia alone.

In those days, there was no direct flight between Phnom Penh and Paris; you had to go to Vietnam and take a ship to Marseilles. As a parting favour, King Sihanouk smoothed my father's journey by lending him a Cessna, a small private plane, and a French military pilot, who flew my father directly to Saigon.

I never saw my father again. Barely two years after his arrival in Paris he fell ill and died, leaving me an orphan at the age of twelve.

So I was brought up by a single mother. She had no profession but was plucky and hard-working. Papa had left her with a small amount of savings, but they melted like snow in the sun. She had five mouths to feed in the house: her aged mother who had no means of her own, an elder daughter (by a Vietnamese father), her two nephews aged four and two, who had been entrusted to her by her sister on her deathbed, and me, her second daughter. All too often she was forced to pull a rabbit from a hat to keep a roof over our heads, feed us all and to provide the four of us with a decent education.

My mother spoke French but couldn't read it. When my father died, she asked a neighbour's husband, Mr. Gauthier, to become my tutor and look after my education. He and his family were refugees from Vietnam and had fled the war in IndoChina. They only stayed in Phnom Penh for a few years before returning to France forever.

Maman was a practising Buddhist; I was a Catholic, baptised at birth, but she never objected to me being brought up as a Christian and our two faiths lived side by side quite happily[3]. For my first communion she wanted to buy me a brand new communion dress, but this turned out to be far too expensive, so my tutor's wife offered to make me one out of her wedding dress. All the same Maman ended up in debt, as she treated me to a small celebration feast of roast chicken, salad and cake.

I did all my schooling at the French Lycée in Phnom Penh, the Lycée Descartes. I never learnt Khmer. I might have looked Vietnamese with my classic *nhac* features inherited from my mother, but I was French and in my heart I felt French[4]. The majority of my classmates were Eurasians like me, although there were a few Vietnamese and French. There were also some Cambodians, the sons or daughters of senior civil servants who could afford to send their children to such an establishment (for us, the half-caste French, school was free). But I didn't spend a lot of time with them. I was very shy and I was never very at ease with other people. I spoke very little Khmer and had no urge to learn it, as I had never thought of Cambodia as my homeland.

I never took a holiday; in July and August I baby-sat for the neighbour in order to pay for my books, pens and paper for the next term. Free time was given over to reading, and preparing for dictations and exercises; I would work with my cousin, sitting on the edge of the bed, leaning on a wooden stool which did for a desk. When my mother couldn't pay

---

3. The nuns who often came to our house were offended by the fact that I ate the offerings that Maman had put on the altar. For the sisters, it was a mortal sin, although my mother saw no harm in it and it seemed perfectly natural to me not to waste food!

4. *Nhac*, diminutive of *nha quê* (countryside), was the term used by French colonists for Vietnamese and meant 'peasant'.

the rent, the landlord cut off the electricity and in the evening we'd finish our homework by moonlight or by the glow of a candle.

We were poor but honest and hardworking. I still admire my mother's heroism. She knew how, come hell or high water, to drum into us the rules of good behaviour and she made enormous sacrifices to put four of us through school. Maybe it was her example that, twenty years later, gave me the moral strength to fight and survive in the hell of the Cambodian forests.

In 1964, I finished my secondary education. When I was twenty, just as I started work, I met the future father of my children, Phou Teang Seng. He was Chinese, from the island of Hainan, whose family had settled in the province of Kampot. I left my mother's house to move in with him in a flat that was partitioned off from the one in which his family lived in – his sister, her husband and their four children, along with their brother, who was a simple-minded boy. We didn't marry; at that time living together was the norm and I didn't want to legalise the situation in case it caused me problems at work - the French Embassy, for example, wouldn't hire French women married to Cambodians or Chinese. At first, I found work as a bilingual French-English typist at the South Korean Consulate. But when diplomatic relations were broken off between South Korea and Cambodia, I left to teach in a private French primary school. I lost this job when I became pregnant because the headmistress, a Frenchwoman, had no health insurance for her staff and didn't want to keep me on in case of an accident. It has to be said that, in Cambodia, we were at the mercy of employers in the private sector. There was no social

security, no health insurance, no pension rights, no ante or
post-natal leave. If you didn't want to lose your job, you had
to work right up to the day before, or even the day of the
birth, and go back two weeks later. We worked more than
forty-five hours a week with only fifteen days of paid holiday
a year. After my daughter Jeannie was born, I found a new
job with a company called Comin Khmer, which was run
by a Dane. Eventually they made me the executive secretary
in a factory, Sokilait, that made condensed milk. I worked
there from the moment the factory was built right through
to the production and launch of the product. Finally, in
1973, I left Sokilait to be the Cultural Attaché's secretary in
the French Embassy in Phnom Penh, a job I held until the
Khmer Rouge came to power.

My husband, Seng, was very entrepreneurial, perhaps a little
too much so. After running the American Officers' Mess in
Phnom Penh, he started all sorts of different businesses and
restaurants. None of them ever worked and we were often
in debt. Then, when the war and bombing began, he found
another line of work, construction. He could have made a
go of it as an architect and decorator, as he was talented
and had extremely good taste. In particular, he designed villas for the nouveau riche of Phnom Penh, who were mostly
Cambodian army officers – generals, colonels and such like,
and he took care of all the interior decoration. This business
did well.

When he was with his military clients, Seng hid his communist sympathies. At home, on the other hand, every day
he'd spout at me, an anti-communist, one of the thoughts
of Chairman Mao. If we started a discussion, we'd inevitably

end up fighting. He was anti-imperialist and anti-capitalist but loved the good life, driving beautiful American cars, eating out in restaurants and drinking good whisky. Quite often I'd be sharp with him and tell him he should go back to China. Of course, this was impossible and he knew it. He was just an armchair communist and anyway, suspicious China didn't want its citizens from overseas back. He was also quite dogmatically anti-Western and he was particularly anti-French. And yet, he chose me ...

That said, we got on well if we avoided politics. He was a good-looking man and I started a family with him. We had three children, Jean-Jacques – born on 25 August 1964, who lived through the Khmer Rouge period from the age of ten to fourteen; Jeannie, born on 30 May 1967, who died of starvation, aged nine, under the Khmer Rouge regime and Françoise, born 19 December 1970, whose premature death a few days later had nothing to do with the Khmer Rouge. My children were recognised by their father, who gave them his surname, but they had French citizenship.

After Jeannie was born, I fell ill. I was so exhausted that I was incapable of looking after the baby. So my husband's aunt, Mme. Champion, who had been married to a Frenchman, looked after her and carried on doing so when I went back to work[5]. Little by little she became her second mother. In the end, Jeannie chose to live with her and only came home for the weekend. If my little Jeannie had stayed at her aunt's that fateful weekend, when Phnom Penh was taken by the Khmer Rouge, two days before Khmer New

---

5. During the 1950s, this aunt lived in Vesoul in France with her husband Lucien Champion, who worked in a mine in Albertville. In 1954, he died in an explosion in the mine. So, three months pregnant and knowing nobody in France, she decided to return to Cambodia.

Year, her fate would have been very different …

But for all its ups and downs, our life was a long tranquil river. It could have and should have flowed on like this in the most unremarkable way in the world, in a land where the sun always shone, peacefully and without any worries. How could one have imagined for a moment that, overnight, on 17 April 1975, it would be plunged into horror?

2/ Tragedy Unfolds: Cambodia 1970-1975

Hell became a reality as early as 1970.

On 18 March 1970, King Norodom Sihanouk, accused of having permitted North Vietnamese troops to set up sanctuaries along the Cambodian-Vietnamese border, is stripped of his role as head of state by General Lon Nol who, with American support, proclaims the Khmer Republic which he leads until 17 April 1975. After the coup d'état, war spreads across the whole of the IndoChinese peninsula. Fear and crime reign in Cambodia. The peaceful Khmer people, a large majority of whom are Buddhist – gentle, smiling believers – will thus become either the victims or perpetrators of appalling, barbarous crimes.

The moment he comes to power, Lon Nol declares war upon the communist Vietnamese forces and denounces the infiltration of Vietcong elements into the country's Vietnamese community;[1] the Ho Chi Minh trail effectively crosses the north-east of Cambodia.[2] The Vietnamese and

---

1. The Vietcong were an armed resistance to the Saigon regime, born out of Vietnam's National Liberation Front.
2. The Ho Chi Minh trail linked the north of Vietnam with the south, passing through Laos and Cambodia. It was made up of a number of paths, channels and pipelines hidden by the forest. The fighters of the Liberation Front (the Vietcong) transported men and materials from the communist north of Vietnam to the zones occupied by their troops in the south. Because of its strategic importance during the Vietnam War, the Ho Chi Minh trail was subjected to incessant American bombing.

those Cambodians of Vietnamese origin were soon subjected to real pogroms on Lon Nol's orders. It's a radical cleanup operation, a wave of barbaric and bloody terror that washes through Cambodian history between 1970 and 1975; it's followed by a tidal wave of Khmer Rouge savagery.

Overnight, all the Vietnamese are arrested and collected together in the north of the city, in hastily created camps in schools and Chinese pagodas, for so-called repatriation to Vietnam, of which there will be none …

The arrests usually take place at night, by surprise. In Phnom Penh, a curfew is ordered; as soon as the lights are out, military trucks trundle heavily through the streets. The residents in my block are of all sorts of origins; Cambodians, Chinese, Vietnamese … but only the Vietnamese are targeted. Every evening, from nightfall onwards, I hear soldiers shouting orders, banging on the front doors of flats with rifle butts – then the cries of distress, the tears of women or children pulled from their sleep and taken away *manu militari*. A sort of Vietnamese witch-hunt is organised. Women no longer dare wear their hair in a traditional Vietnamese bun and cut it very short to look more like Cambodians. Overnight, all my Vietnamese friends are forced to flee the country. It is the prelude to a nightmare.[3]

The Vietnamese leave in a rush and can only take a few personal belongings; they have to abandon everything. Houses, furniture and anything else left behind is confiscated by the state or pillaged by dishonest neighbours. Some manage to sell their things in haste, but for a pittance; they

---

3. My Vietnamese mother was not worried by Lon Nol's troops, because she fell under my responsibility; as a French citizen I could vouch for her. On top of that, many of the senior figures of the Cambodian regime had known my father well, the majority of them having been his pupils at the Lycée Sisowath.

are easy prey for profiteers of all sorts ... Panic sets in even among those Vietnamese who are naturalised Khmer citizens or are married to Cambodians. With checks on every street corner, they no longer feel safe and they no longer dare to go outside.

The makeshift camps are soon full. With the heat and the poor hygiene, children and the elderly are the first victims of epidemics, particularly cholera or dysentery. Next come the systematic massacres; all those trying to reach Vietnam by boat are slaughtered, their bodies thrown unceremoniously into the water. Women are raped; Buddhist monks and nuns, accused of collaborating with the Viêtcong, are exterminated; their pagodas ransacked and burned. An elderly friend of my mother, a nun in a pagoda in Kompong Speu province, has her throat savagely slit.

The Lon Nol years also see Cambodia sucked inexorably into the war in IndoChina. North Vietnamese troops intervene in the country, which is pounded by American air power ... It's during this period that the Khmer Rouge start peddling their nationalist movement in the countryside, rallying the young and mostly illiterate peasantry to their cause and creating an army.

In Phnom Penh, since the proclamation of the Khmer Republic, skirmishes between pro-American government soldiers and the Khmer Rouge rebels take place every day; war devours the country ...

Faced with a situation that is deteriorating daily, conscription is introduced in June 1970. The new regime needs cannon fodder. Rich and well-to-do Cambodians hurry to send their children overseas (to France or the United States), on the pretext that they can continue their studies ... but in reality it's to escape military service and death, because at home large numbers of young conscripts are being killed each day on the battlefields.

Added to the fear of conscription is that of the rockets raining down on the town night and day sowing terror. These murderous shells target not just schools, cinemas and markets, but also the hospitals, already full of the sick and wounded. Twice, the playgrounds of nursery schools are hit and many children are killed. The city falls prey to mass panic.

The Khmer Rouge have no difficulty in sapping the morale of the inhabitants, who soon realise that those in charge are simply incapable, ineffective puppets in the pay of the Americans. Added to this incompetence are greed and corruption. The latter is of such magnitude that Lon Nol's government rapidly becomes unpopular. The United States finances the war effort without counting the cost, but top civil servants and military men cash in hugely by exaggerating the numbers of soldiers in order to pocket their pay or by establishing lists of phantom dead soldiers to get their hands on their 'widows" pensions, or even to resell their arms to the enemy. With this easy money, they live like kings; fun and restaurants, sumptuous villas equipped with air-conditioning and the most up-to-date hi-fi systems; these are the new rich Phnompenhois.

Of course, this depravity doesn't lead to victory. Contrary to the deliberately reassuring tone of the constant radio broadcasts and despite the massive American military and economic aid, Lon Nol's troops suffer defeat after defeat and lose ground day by day.

Between 1971 and 1975, the massive influx of refugees from neighbouring provinces conquered and occupied by

the Khmer Rouge means that the population of Phnom
Penh almost triples, to between two and three million inhabitants.

Little by little the capital begins to suffocate. The supply
of staple goods becomes more and more difficult as the main
roads are cut. The Tonlé Sap, the only river that crosses the
country and along which fuel and other vital raw materials are transported, is harassed daily by the enemy. A large
number of merchant ships and tankers are sunk, meaning
stocks of all sorts of things run out and there's a mind-
boggling leap in the price of essentials such as rice, sugar,
salt, raw materials for the manufacture of condensed milk,
petrol, etc. Speculation is rife. The local currency, the *riel*,
is hardly worth anything. Bank notes are now nothing but
paper; to do one's daily shopping, you have to set off with a
basketful of notes.

The rich rush to buy gold and hard currency, bought at
exorbitant rates, to stash them safely abroad. On the eve of
the city's fall, a French franc is worth 560 *riels* on the black
market, the US dollar 2,500 *riels* and a tael of gold (36g)
450,000 *riels*. Those who want to leave the country can negotiate an exit visa for around 700,000 *riels* and air tickets
are subject to last minute surcharges that are beyond reach.
The airport, however, is also a target for rocket attacks which
often stop the planes from taking off altogether.

In April 1975, Lon Nol's pro-American government falls;
it's hung on for five years. The last days of the regime are
grim. You can feel it dying; the streets are deserted from
seven in the evening, as soon as the curfew starts. The inhabitants seal themselves in their houses, frightened of the rockets, and have no more than two or three hours of electricity

and running water a day because of fuel shortages. Little by little foreigners leave the country.

What should we do? Which saint should we turn to? The Cambodians curse Lon Nol and his band of puppets. They desire only one thing, peace, and wish for the victory of the Khmer Rouge whom they think will liberate them from the yoke of the American stooges and finally put an end to their troubles.

Unfortunately, they don't know ... not yet, that the word 'liberation' will be forever engraved in their history as a synonym for a stream of macabre evil: imprisonment, mental and physical torture, summary executions, massacres, forced labour, families separated, famine, death ... They cannot imagine that these so-called liberators, the Khmer Rouge, who are mostly uneducated, will systematically eliminate other Khmers, their own brothers, whom they consider to be rotten citizens, corrupted by imperialists; that they will get rid of all foreigners, regardless of race (French, Chinese or Vietnamese), with no regard for age or religion (Muslims, known locally as *Chams*, Catholics and Buddhists), that they will organise the most brutal and radical reconstruction of society that has ever been attempted in order to construct a new, pure nation. They don't know that absolutely everyone will be submitted to an infernal and pitiless lottery designed to sort the wheat from the chaff, that those who escape the first wave of executions will be slowly decimated in turn by forced labour, deprivation, sickness, lack of medical care and medicines. They do not know that their country is going to be transformed into a gigantic agricultural co-operative dominated by the peasantry, under the aegis of a bloodthirsty madman, a Maoist extremist exponent of the agricultural revolution and with the open support of the communist Chinese!

In 1975, the Cambodian people still know nothing of this. They are happy to hope and, irony of ironies, to pray to Buddha for the victory of the enemy.

3/ The City Empties Out

In the cultural section of the French Embassy where I work, there is no place for hope. Every day we receive alarming reports from AFP, the French news agency, of fighting in the provinces, the destruction of towns and villages and people on the move.

When I share this information with my husband, he doesn't believe a word of it. As far as he's concerned, it's imperialist propaganda; he listens secretly to *Radio Peking* every evening, which ceaselessly proclaims the victory of the Khmer revolutionary troops, saying that, wherever they go, peace returns and the people live happily ... Seng, a confirmed Maoist and communist idealist partisan – in theory – repeats tirelessly to anyone who wants to listen that communists are not savages, that they have laws, and that we can trust them! He really believes this is a truth set in stone. When I think of the fate that awaited him, I still mourn his pigheadedness and his infatuation with such beliefs.

The authorities at the French Embassy urge me, like all the other employees, to leave the country. But the French administration will only pay the travel expenses for me and my children ... not those of their father, as he's a foreigner, nor, naturally, those of my in-laws. I find myself facing a tragic dilemma; we can't afford to pay for extra air tickets

16

and I cannot face leaving the father of my children and his family to the horrors of war. What will happen if the Khmer Rouge wins the war? The unknown worries and frightens me, but I tell myself that life will surely return to normal. Maybe Seng is right and we shouldn't give in to panic ...

My conscience stops me from following the advice of the French authorities, who are slowly repatriating all their nationals (experts, aid workers, teachers, doctors, etc ...). On 15 March 1975, the first contingent leave on a military Transal destined for Bangkok, a second contingent on 30 March, then a third at the beginning of April. Certain Cambodian personalities and some foreign diplomats, who are still stuck here, are able to take advantage of these evacuations by paying their way. With a heavy heart, I watch my colleagues pack their bags one after another, all the while telling myself, in order to keep my spirits up, that peace will return.

Before leaving their posts, the Chargé d'Affaires and the Cultural Attaché urge me for the last time to get out with my children. Seng, whose ideas are redder than the Reds themselves, convinces me, with his blind optimism, to do otherwise: "The Government troops will surrender, it'll be the end of civil war and all will go back to normal, you'll see ... "

Michel Deverge, the Cultural Attaché, comes up with another solution; he'll take Jean-Jacques and Jeannie to Paris and look after them until the situation settles down and I can either join them or bring them home if peace returns. Seng categorically refuses. Under no circumstances does he want to be separated from his children. It's human and I understand him. But selfishly, he also says that if ever some-

17

thing happens to us … but nothing is going to happen … well, if ever … well, then everyone will die together and that will be that!

Perhaps the children should have left. To this day I still frequently recall his words with bitterness. Alas, what for? The deed is done …

Twenty-five years later, my heart broken and bruised, I still cry for my dear lost ones, especially my daughter Jeannie. But, paradoxical as it is, I regret it a little less that I stayed. In France, I have met up with several French friends, Eurasian women like me, who, on the day of the exodus, wanted to leave Cambodia with their native-born husbands and took refuge in the French Embassy. They were admitted, but alone with their children, while their husbands of Cambodian or Chinese nationality were turned away, tossed back into the inferno as unsavoury, under the pretext that the Khmer Rouge were watching the Embassy. Today these women are safe and sound but lack peace of mind and are far from happy. Some of them have found out that their husbands perished in the hell, others don't know what became of them. Such a situation would have filled me with remorse and seems to me far crueller. Due to force of circumstance, I followed Phou Teang Seng, but miraculously came out of it, with my son, and I was able to see and live through all that really happened right up to the end, without, to my eternal sorrow, being able to help those close to me who lost their lives. What pains me more than anything else is the death of my darling, fragile nine-year-old daughter from starvation.

April 1975. While the rats flee the sinking ship, I stay steady at my post in the cultural section right up until Saturday 12, the eve of the holiday of *Chaul Chhnam*, the Cambodian New Year, according to the Khmer lunar calendar. That day, an atmosphere of general panic reigns across Phnom Penh; there's an incessant dance of military helicopters, and ambulance sirens ferrying help to the wounded. That very morning, rockets again fall on several parts of the town, one close to the French Embassy, killing and wounding. The shops and grocers are closed because they've run out of supplies, or because the owners have already packed their bags. You can see looting everywhere that has been abandoned. When I go back to work at midday, I discover that the American Embassy is evacuating its entire staff by helicopter. What should I do? Should we go too? Yes, but where to? Besides, it's already too late. Stay then? Yes, but what will happen?

My daughter Jeannie reluctantly comes to spend the week-end with us. Ah! If only that day she had stayed at her great–aunt's, she would have been able to leave the capital with her, westwards and without doubt she would still be alive … since during the exodus, the aunt took jewellery with her, which she was able to exchange for rice. Besides that, she only had two mouths to feed; her's and her son's, whereas we were nine in all. They both got out and live in France today. I have seen the old lady since. It's impossible to console her over the fate of her great-niece, my daughter. She still cries about it and reproaches me for her death.

Alas, one cannot undo the past. So on Saturday 12 April, Jeannie arrives to spend the week-end with us, her parents, who, without knowing, without wanting it, are going to lead her to her tragic and ill-fated destiny– hunger then death.

On the morning of Sunday 26 April, the military headquarters are bombed and a general curfew is decreed for the whole day. Fortunately, we did all our shopping for the weekend and the New Year the evening before. In spite of the feeling outside that the world is coming to an end, to keep our spirits up we decide to celebrate the New Year with a group of friends and Cambodian neighbours from the same building, not knowing that this will be the last one for a long time. We dine by candlelight, as the electricity has been cut off since the middle of the afternoon. Everyone has brought some of their own supplies. At the end of the evening, we are astonished to discover that the radio has stopped broadcasting any news, so we decide to go up on the roof terrace of our building to see what's going on around us. Faced with the nightmarish spectacle before us, we realise that Lon Nol's troops have capitulated. Phnom Penh is plunged into darkness; in the north of the capital, about five kilometres away, the petrol refinery is ablaze, as are many warehouses and munitions depots. There are distant explosions. The capital is dying but, oddly, everyone feels relieved, reassured, and almost happy. Some even ask Buddha to ensure the Khmer Rouge troops are victorious! As for me, I pray to the Good Lord that peace will return very soon.

The next day, Monday 17 April, without any precise information as there is still no radio, I get ready for work as usual, keen to get fresh news from the Embassy. But just as I get into my car, the sound of exploding hand grenades or firecrackers resonates around me, then gunshots, very close this time and coming from all sides. The Khmer Rouge are entering the capital and making their presence known by firing their guns.

Then a huge din starts up. From every house cries of joy burst forth, and in our street I distinctly hear the cheer:

"*Cheyo yautheas pakdevat!*" ("Long live the revolutionary soldiers!"). The month of April is very hot and very dry. Curious to see what is happening outside, I jump out of the car to have a look and am transfixed by the sight; men, women and children clapping and shouting in unison: "*Cheyo yautheas pakdevat!*". They rush to get in front of their blessed liberators, to welcome them and offer them something to drink. The town is delirious. The warriors are dressed in a black uniform, wearing black caps, with red and white chequered scarves around their necks and, on their feet, 'Ho Chi Minh sandals' made of recycled rubber from car tyres.[1] Most of the *yautheas* are very young, almost kids.[2] They seem decent and very proud of their victory and happy to be in Phnom Penh. They are armed to the teeth; just the sight of them gives me goose pimples. I see my daft husband again, heading off to cheer them, welcoming them to the street with an armload of bottles of Tsin Tao beer. They accept the drinks as if it's their right, with no thanks to anyone, already giving the disagreeable impression that they're the masters of the place.

Twenty–four hours after their arrival everyone is disenchanted, and the euphoria of the previous day quickly fades away as the soldiers whom they've welcomed triumphantly begin to go down every street, into every house handing out 'firm' orders to leave Phnom Penh. "You must evacuate the town," they tell us, "just for two or three days ... as Angkar wants you to be safe from the American air raids." (Angkar? Who is Angkar? What does that mean? I later learn that it means the 'the Organisation' or 'the Party' – all those en-

---

1. These sandals, worn by Ho Chi Minh, the Vietnamese communist revolutionary leader, were adopted by the fighters of the Vietcong.
2. Yauthea is the term used by the Khmer Rouge for a soldier.

dowed with power to run a village, or a team of workers, speak in its name; Angkar is everywhere). "Just take the bare minimum, lock your doors carefully and give us the keys. We'll look after your things until you come back. Don't worry, leave in peace."

Everyone follows these orders scrupulously. Disconcerted by the turn of events which no one was expecting, we carry them out without wasting time and Seng, the children, my in-laws and I pack our bags. We do well, as we later learn that those who didn't want to leave their homes were accused of treason and all massacred on the spot.

Early in the morning, my sister-in-law's husband leaves to see his parents who live in the west of town. We'll never hear a word from him again. My mother was living quite close by in the same area. Unfortunately, as I was stuck with the children, I couldn't go and see her – if I had set out alone, I would definitely have been separated from my children ...

We take rice, salt, sugar, dried fish, medicines, mosquito nets, mats to sleep on, candles, cigarettes, a bottle of Johnnie Walker whiskey for Seng, a change of clothes, school books so the children can do their homework, and of course, all our identity papers and cash (around two million *riels* exchanged a few days earlier). We take good care to leave a little stock of rice, dried fish, salt, sugar and coffee for our return, in case the shops don't reopen immediately. Poor trusting idiots that we are! Before leaving, my husband gives the keys of our apartments to the *yautheas*, thanking them for their kind assistance. Today, thinking back, I tell myself that these monsters must have really been mocking us. To chase us from our homes under the pretext of protecting us and pretending to care for our houses was the first grotesque lie of this invisible and omnipresent Angkar ... but not the last. We shall discover throughout our Calvary that all Angkar's promises will be nothing but lies.

So, around nine in the morning, we leave the town with our big Chevrolet filled to the brim with luggage. In the back seat, my sister-in-law Li and her four children – three girls; Leng, eighteen-years-old, Hoa, sixteen-years-old, Phan, twelve-years-old, and a boy, Ha, who's five. In the front seat, next to Seng, who's at the wheel, I put my son Jean-Jacques, aged ten, and take seven-year-old Jeannie on my lap. Seng's youngest brother, a big, rather simple boy, prefers to follow us on his bike, towing behind him the henhouse in which are two hens and a duck. In the general panic, we quickly lose sight of him and never see him again. We try to get to the French Embassy in the north of Phnom Penh. But this proves impossible, as the town has been divided into four by soldiers manning road blocks; residents of the northern sector must evacuate to the north, those of the east to the east, etc. We are in the southern sector.

As soon as I'm outside, I'm frozen in terror by the desolate spectacle in front of me and burst into tears. A stream of men, women, old people and children are hurrying past jostling, pushing or pulling carts full of furniture and baggage. It's barely ten in the morning but the sun is already beating down; it's a blazing sun and there's a clammy heat. Those without cars or carts have to evacuate on foot; the mothers carry babies on their backs, while the bigger ones, barefoot, run behind crying. The husbands carry belongings and food on *palanches* (bamboo sticks balanced across their shoulders from which wicker baskets full of their food and possessions dangle on either side), old people struggle to keep up with the young. The roads are crowded with bikes, bicycle rickshaws, cars crawling at walking pace – those who are lucky enough to still have a bit of petrol; those who don't have a drop left in their tanks are towed or pushed by the adults. Even the hospitals are emptied and with no consideration the sick are thrown into the throng, lying on stretchers, the transfusion equipment still attached to their arms. The insane, freed from their asylums, have no idea what's happening and laugh or mumble incomprehensibly. Prisoners, drunk with their new found liberty, seize the opportunity to pillage everything on the way; houses, grocers, second hand stores, the 7-Up float. It's all go.

To reassure myself I repeat: "It's only a nightmare, Denise, a bad dream, nothing but a bad dream; you are going to wake up … "

My communist-junkie tries to calm me down; he tells me there's nothing to be afraid of: "Don't worry. They're doing the right thing. It's normal that they want to protect us from the air raids. We have to make their task of cleaning up the town easier; they'll let us come back afterwards." This blind trust, this blissful optimism in this faithless, lawless regime still staggers me today.

In the throng, I quickly spot the refugees who have already been evacuated from a town or a village; they've only brought food supplies and, above all, as much rice as possible. Townies like us have no idea what awaits us. Many are laden with mattresses, furniture, radios, banknotes (money which will soon be the cause of many suicides) – in short, useless things that will be progressively confiscated from us during our journey. Since the beginning of the war between the soldiers of Lon Nol and the Khmer Rouge, refugees have arrived daily in Phnom Penh and, at the time of the general evacuation, the entire population has risen to around three million people.

Three million people thrown onto the streets overnight; three million people, frightened, exhausted by the April heat, three million human beings walking towards the unknown; yes, the complete unknown, and this uncertainty is very difficult to bear. We don't know what's happening, or what's going to happen; we don't know where we are going; we have no precise instructions. Each group of *yautheas* on bikes whom we come across is happy enough just to shout: "Don't worry about your houses, we'll look after them, continue in this direction. Angkar is waiting for you there, Angkar will meet you. Angkar will take care of you. Don't be afraid! You'll be back in two or three days." They're lying and they'll lie to the end of hell.

We're advancing at a walking pace when a group of three Khmer Rouge soldiers in green uniforms, carrying bags of medicines and various articles stolen from a second-hand shop and a chemist, stop our car and ask my husband to let them get in. The latter, still in shock at his 'liberation' and deeply thankful to those who have just freed him from the yoke of the pro-American regime, greets them eagerly:

"Where are you going and how far?"

"About twenty kilometres south of Phnom Penh."

Seng tells them he has only a few litres of fuel left. So while two of them go off, we wait patiently under the other's watch. Half an hour later they come back from who knows where with a jerry can of petrol. For almost five years, fuel has been scarce. You have to buy it on the black market at an inflated price and it's often mixed with kerosene. At the

Embassy, I get a monthly ration in coupons and we fill up at the diplomatic pump.

Once the tank is full, the soldiers rudely order me to get into the back seat with my two children, while the two of them squeeze into the front next to Seng and the third climbs onto the roof with their booty and orders us to drive on. He then clears the road by firing his gun in the air. The grown-ups keep quiet; only Ha and Jeannie, frightened by the gunfire and uncomfortable in the crush and the heat, start to cry. Li and I do our best to calm them, convinced that these young soldiers are doing us a favour by helping us to get out of town faster.

Thus, our car leaves the south of Phnom Penh without too much trouble, albeit slowly. As we pass by Chamcar Mon, the residence of the head of state, a terrible stench begins to make my stomach heave. As we near the palace, I see dozens, maybe more – I haven't the courage to count them – of corpses of government soldiers, scattered, lying on the ground, swollen and starting to decompose in the sun. Our Khmer Rouge 'hitchhikers' say absolutely nothing, and squashed in the back between our luggage and the rest of my family, I tremble and cry in silence.

The heat inside the car is overwhelming. We drive for hours with all the windows down, as far as the edge of town to a suburb called Takhmau. There, there's the first road-block, manned by black-clad Khmer Rouge, and the first search; they make us get out of the car and demand our identity papers. Our three hitchhikers don't move – they haven't said a word since the beginning of the trip. Extremely calm and totally confident, my husband gets out all the papers and official documents that we have in our possession (identity cards, the children's birth certificates, my French Embassy identity card and my French passport), explaining that the children and I are French. The Khmer Rouge stare at us viciously and contemptuously confiscate all the documents and rip them into tiny pieces without even looking at them – like most of the Khmer Rouge, they don't know how to read – and toss them in the air. "From now on, there are no more Chinese or French or Vietnamese, we're all Khmer brothers, and we'll only speak one language, Khmer." Stunned, I eye the remnants of my identity tossed aside like confetti. And in bewilderment, I then notice that there are banknotes on the ground, all different denominations, but mostly 500 *riels*. The street is littered with them. Laughing menacingly the *yautheas* explain that since 17 April 1975, the date of their victory, "Nols (they use a derogatory term for Lon Nol), are no longer valid currency in the *dey romdoch* (the liberated zone)."

Once the search is over, they give us the signal to continue our journey southwards. I'm more and more desperate and consumed with worry while my sister-in-law is completely calm. She too is an enthusiastic communist idealist and, at this moment, she seems to have total confidence in what is going on.

In our misery, we have nevertheless – thanks to the 'invaluable' help of the soldiers who have requisitioned our car – managed to leave the capital without too much trouble. For those on foot, bicycle or in carts, the physical effort needed to carry the children and their bundles adds to their emotional shock. The oppressive, humid heat is hideously tiring, especially for children and old people, who weaken rapidly. As we move southwards, we see from time to time on the edge of the road the bodies of people who have died from exhaustion, or of those who, in despair, have given in to death. But nobody has the time or the inclination to stop and bury them. The motto of the moment is: "Everyone for himself and Buddha for all." This desolate spectacle over-whelms me; I weep and inwardly curse Seng for having got us into all this. But this nightmarish day trip is only just beginning. We will be immersed in it for four years, four years that will seem to me like four centuries.

Around three in the afternoon, we arrive at a village called Svay Aloum, about twenty-five kilometres from Phnom Penh. Our hitchhiker-soldiers order us to stop; they get out, unload their booty and climb into a canoe moored on the banks of the Tonlé Sap, which we've been following since Takhmau. Before leaving us, they simply say: "From now on, keep going south, Angkar awaits you." No thanks, no goodbyes.

Angkar, more Angkar, always Angkar … From now on, we hear nothing but this each time there are orders or changes to the rules of our new life. The children are tired – breakfast was a long time ago and they begin to get hungry and thirsty. The youngest, Jeannie and Ha, start snivelling again. We decide to stop to eat in the shade of a mango tree. We still have a little dried fish and some rice, and everyone is happy to have something to eat.

Contrary to what the *yautheas* have told us, we discover that not far away, in Kien Svay, money is still in use and that one can get hold of fruit, vegetables and other foodstuffs. Perhaps the villagers don't know what's going on. Out of curiosity, Seng decides to go there with 100,000 *riels*. After a while, he comes back with 200 grams of soy sauce that have cost him 30,000 *riels*, a kilo of cucumbers for 20,000 *riels* and 300 grams of pork for 50,000 *riels*. What exorbitant prices! There's no doubt about it, the old money is losing all its value, and food becomes almost priceless. A few days later, there won't be a single place in the country where you can use the banknotes that until now have been in circulation. But all the same, we'll continue to look after our remaining million *riels* carefully, in the foolish hope that everything will soon return to normal.

After this short break, we take to the road again as far as Prey Touch, but we run out of petrol at the edge of the village, right in front of a gang of *yautheas*. A new search, new confiscations – this time it's the children's school books, two or three books and magazines in French, our watches and the cassettes from the car radio that disappear. "You won't need to read or listen to music any more, you won't speak French or Chinese any more, we'll all speak one single language, Khmer." At that moment, the only thought upsetting me is that the children won't be able to work. I've no idea yet of the far more tragic fate that's in store for them. When they consider that they have fleeced us sufficiently, the *yautheas* give us the order to continue, to carry on heading south. But since we don't have any petrol left, the only way to proceed is to push the car.

Fortunately, the sun is less fierce and, as night falls, we arrive at the pagoda of Prey Touch, which is already three-quarters full of refugees. The monks are still there; they hand out a little rice mixed with ground corn and a mess tin of green papaya soup. A frugal but much needed meal – the children can eat, and we are happy to make do with their leftovers. After we've eaten, we try to question the people around us who are getting ready to leave again, but they don't know much about what is going on either. What is sure is that we still haven't arrived at our destination, we must simply carry on; but where to? Nobody knows. It's at this point that we bump into a neighbour from our apartment block who, seeing we've got a problem with the car, offers to tow us.

So we get back on the road. Very late at night, we arrive at another village, where the old Khmer chief, who hasn't been completely converted by living in the Khmer Rouge 'liberated zone' since 1972, gives us an affable welcome. He gives us a snack and allows us to camp underneath his house on stilts. He is a *Khmer romdoch*, a free Khmer. Like other Cambodians, he's been brainwashed by the Khmer Rouge, of course, but his age grants him a certain amount of insight and compassion towards his fellow man.

The two little ones are exhausted and have long been fast asleep. We're content to be able to finally doze off, even if it's on the ground, with no mosquito nets, squashed one against another on a hastily laid out mat.

The following day, on 19 April, we have to get going at first light, on empty stomachs. The children, especially the little ones, start to moan. Faced with their tears, the old man gives us a bunch of bananas and a few ripe papayas, all the while advising – his face filled with pity as if he knows what's waiting for us – "Keep going a little bit longer, my children, Angkar is expecting you … " Still towed by our neighbour, we arrive in the late morning at Tukveal, about forty-eight kilometres from Phnom Penh. We stop at a pagoda where numerous refugees are already camping and decide to stay there until the following morning. In reality, we still don't know what to do or where to go, in fact no one knows any different, and Angkar appears more invisible than ever ...

Opposite, on the other side of the Tonlé Sap river, we see an island, Koh Tukveal. [3]

On the morning of 20 April, after a frugal breakfast, we consider moving on. As we start loading our mats into the car, Koh Tukveal's village chief arrives, a certain Mr Thiên. He's accompanied by three henchmen, all dressed in black, with black caps, the red and white check scarf rolled around their necks and 'Ho Chi Minh sandals' on their feet. Mr Thiên is also a Khmer, who has been living in the 'liberated zone' since 1970. There seems little to incline him towards compassion in his steely look. With his acolytes, he inspects the refugees' appearance, measuring them up by what they possess and quickly picks out the better off – those who have a car. He gives us all a sign to line up and explains that we are going to Koh Tukveal. Canoes already await the chosen families, who now have to submit to a new search before embarking, and fresh confiscations, "as a security measure". Anything that interests the Khmer Rouge disappears rapidly into their pockets; jewellery, eau de cologne, bars of soap, medicine, syringes and thermometers. I manage to hide a few things in a basket. But the pretty doll that Jeannie is holding in her arms, last year's Christmas present from the French Embassy to the children of their employees, is torn brutally from her arms, despite her tears and wails. Tears in my eyes, I implore Mr Thiên to let her keep it, but he's inflexible and replies dryly that children will have no more

---

3. *Koh* means "island".

need of toys and that, in any case, there will be no more time to play because there will be other things to do. With a heavy heart, powerless, I can only try and console my little girl as best as I can. At this moment, I still don't understand the message that these monsters want to get across: "Don't hold onto your material possessions, you'll have no need of them. Soon you'll need just a change of clothes, a mess tin and a spoon and nothing else, because Angkar's watching over you and will provide you with everything!" I feel like I've been stabbed in the heart each time that they confiscate a memento or something personal; but as we are progressively forced into hell, stripped of everything, all that counts is food and survival.

Before we set sail, the Khmer Rouge demands that my husband hands over the car keys. They tell him that Angkar needs it: "Angkar is borrowing it from you and will give it back to you when you go back to Phnom Penh." Another lie, another load of trickery that Seng, always proud to be able to be of service to this invisible and omnipotent Angkar, swallows without a shadow of a doubt.

4/ The First Camp: Koh Tukveal

Along with several other families from Phnom Penh, including the neighbours who had towed us, I take my place in the canoes, my throat choked with anxiety despite Seng's calm. The crossing doesn't take long and after a few minutes we disembark on the island and discover a little village of straw huts on stilts, surrounded by banana trees, sugar cane and cornfields that stretch as far as the eye can see. A list in hand, Mr Thiên distributes the families amongst the villagers. We are singled out for special treatment; instead of being parachuted into a local family, Mr Thiên issues us with an empty hut right next door to his own. My husband interprets this as a mark of distinction, although this is, in fact, just a way of keeping an eye on us and, above all, to be in a position to confiscate all our goods of any value.

Thiên is a small man with fine features, without doubt a half-caste Chinese. He's friendly towards us, a little too much so for my taste, and I fear his false kindness will be our downfall. His mother, an old lady of eighty, by contrast shows genuine kindness towards the refugees. "My poor children, my poor children, I pity you ..." she often says, knowing what fate awaits us. But she dares not talk; she too is spied on by her own children. From this moment onwards, I have to adapt to a new life – a life without comfort, the

33

moon and candles taking the place of electricity, the river that of running water. We are without shoes, etc.

For our first meal in our new residence, Mr Thiên gives us a small saucepan of fish soup and a mess tin of rice mixed with corn that we share with my sister-in-law and her four children. Fortunately, there are still some bananas and a papaya left. At sunset, exhausted, we hurry to bed. We unroll the mats on the floor of the hut. It's made of bamboo slats bound together with creeper. Before sinking into a disturbed sleep haunted by dreams, I pray to the Good Lord that he will quickly put an end to this.

At six in the morning, we are dragged from our sleep by the ringing of a bell; the village chief's son – who I later learn is also a spy, a *schlop* – sounds the roll call. Young and old must assemble in front of the chief's house. The Tonlé Sap runs close to the hut – I run to it quickly and clean myself up. The children, woken up so brutally, begin to cry. Jeannie asks for milk; the last carton was drunk on the journey. Desperate, I start blaming my husband again; why didn't he listen to me? Why did he drag us here? When Mr Thiên's mother hears the little ones' tears, she gives us a bowl of rice with some grilled, salted fish; this will be Jeannie and Ha's last breakfast. From the next day, due to short supplies, we'll have to get used to having only two meals a day.

Once all the new arrivals are gathered, Mr Thiên preaches, for the first time, the ten commandments of Angkar that must be learned by heart:

- Everyone will be reformed by work.
- Do not steal.
- Always tell the truth to Angkar.

- Obey Angkar whatever the circumstances.

- It is forbidden to show feelings; joy or sadness.

- It is forbidden to be nostalgic about the past – the spirit must not *vivoat* (stray).

- It is forbidden to beat children, as from now on they are the children of Angkar.

- The children will be educated by Angkar.

- Never complain about anything.

- If you commit an act in contradiction to the line set forth by Angkar you will publicly self-criticise yourself at the daily indoctrination meetings, that are compulsory for everyone.

Mr Thiên explains in Khmer. I understand what he says, but as I can neither read nor write the language, I have to write down the sounds I've heard phonetically in order to memorise this lesson in correct behaviour, which from now on, we will have to recite at every meeting.

Next it's the instructions concerning our appearance:

- We will never again wear coloured clothes.

- We will dye all our clothes black, with the juice of a fruit called *makhoeur*, which grows on the island. To do this we must pound the fruit, extract the juice, then boil the clothes in it for about an hour.

- Women must cut their nails and their hair. Long, manicured nails are out of the question; hair must be short and cropped.

- We will walk barefoot; no shoes or sandals.

- People with bad eyesight will no longer be allowed to wear their spectacles as they will no longer be necessary.

- When you are seated on a bench or chair it is forbidden to cross your legs, as this is an outward sign of capitalism.

Then he explains our new way of life; working hours and the new terms to adopt in everyday language:

- You will work every day from sunrise to sunset; Saturdays, Sundays and public holidays are abolished and the work will be shared out in the following fashion:

- As it's the season, women will plant the corn. The men will clear the land that is still overgrown with scrub or trees; they will be replaced by sugar cane.

- In order to help Angkar economise, there will be no more than two meals a day; at midday and in the evening.

- Trade no longer exists; there is nothing to buy, nothing to sell. Angkar will distribute our rice ration every day and one tin of condensed milk per family, per week (which we'll never set eyes on). For the rest, we must fend for ourselves.

- When saying 'to eat', the expression *pisa bai* is forbidden, from now on, *say hôp bai*.[1]

- The titles 'Mr.' and 'Mrs.' are abolished; everyone will call each other *mit* or comrade, (*mit* for a man, *mit neary* for a married woman and *neary* for a young girl).

- Everyone will speak Khmer. It is forbidden to speak French, Chinese or Vietnamese.

After this address, the rest of the first day is given over to putting the new orders into practice. The village women cut our hair. While I watch my long tresses being hacked off with a rusty pair of scissors, I can't stop crying, but later on when I have no soap or shampoo and my head is covered with lice, I'll be happy to have a completely shaved head.

---

1. The two expressions both mean 'to eat' but *pisa bai* was used by bourgeois and intellectuals under the old regime, above all when addressing an older or respected person. The expression *hôp bai* was imposed by the Khmer Rouge to wipe out social distinctions based on age.

Then they show us where to find the trees with the *makhoeur* to dye the clothes. To pick them we must beat the branches with a long bamboo stick, then crush the fruit in a mortar, and finally find containers big enough to dye our clothes in. Nothing is free; the women bargain their help and information for medicine or rice. From now on, rice, salt, sugar and medicine become the most valuable currency. I learn this bit by bit as I get dragged down into hell.

From the second day, everyone is set to work. We have to adapt, and fast! For those of us, like me, who know nothing of working the fields, and have never lived in the countryside, the hard labour begins. The villagers hand out pickaxes to the men and take them to the other side of the island to start clearing the land. The village women gather the women and children and take them into the fields that have already been ploughed to sow the corn.

How do you walk barefoot, on ploughed earth, baked and hardened by the sun, when you aren't used to it? The first day it is martyrdom each time I put one foot in front of the other in the furrows. The heartless villagers mock me viciously: "Look how those townies walk!" They imitate me. I try to stay calm, but tears flood into my eyes ... but no, you cannot cry under any circumstances. That's been spelt out – even if you lose a loved one. I have to admit that not all the Phnompenhois are as useless as me; some of them are originally from the countryside and for them walking barefoot comes naturally.

In the days that follow, we learn how to plant seeds of corn in the earth, placing three or four in each hole at spaces of thirty or forty centimetres. I also have to learn how to draw water from the river, then to water the furrows with the filled buckets that hang from a yoke across my shoulders.

From the age of eight, children will take part in all the chores. The youngest, in this case Jeannie and Ha, will stay in the house all day. Two or three times a week, they go to look for firewood for cooking, with other children their age. There is no question of playing – they are capable of work, and Angkar is in charge of making them realise this. The Khmer Rouge think the children are like blank sheets of paper on which they can print whatever they want. In very little time, Angkar will remould our childrens' spirits and instil its ideology. These monsters will use the children to spy on the adults, their parents, who are regarded as rotten, corrupt and beyond redemption. Angkar's goal is to create a new nation, with the good seeds that they will keep after they've sifted out the bad pennies.

After the first day's work, I am so tired and stiff that I can barely swallow my precious bowl of rice. It's precious because it's the last bowl of good white rice we'll be allowed. From tomorrow it'll be consistently mixed with corn. Angkar has supply problems, so we must tighten our belts and feed the children first.

Within a few weeks both the young and old lose several kilos. The children no longer have any vitality, no inclination to play or to laugh. My husband, by nature quite robust, used to his daily whisky and his cigarettes, sees his spare tyre melt away in the space of a few days and must submit to a diet of rainwater and bartered tobacco, rolled in dried banana leaves. His face wrinkles quite noticeably.

One morning, some days after our arrival on the island of Tukveal, we are summoned to the pagoda on the mainland. Everybody must celebrate the victory and liberation of the country by the courageous *yautheas*! So off we go with our packed lunch in a mess tin made of palm leaves, called a *smok*. We get back into the canoes to cross back over the river.

Thinking we're returning home, the children seem quite happy ... as for myself, I am hoping in secret; after all, there have been rumours going around that Angkar will send the population back home.

The pagoda fills up rapidly, as refugees stream in from all sides. The 'audience' obediently sits right down on the floor and waits patiently for Angkar's arrival. At last they appear ... in the form of a group of three or four men, dressed in black pyjamas, with those unmistakeable red and white chequered scarves around their necks and their Ho Chi Minh sandals. One of them, who appears to be the leader, begins a long speech in praise of the *yautheas pakdevat*, the soldiers of the revolution, and recalls the history of Cambodia from the reign of King Sihanouk up to the victory of the Khmer Rouge:

"Comrades, before our victory we asked those of you who were foreigners to leave the capital and our compatriots to join the Liberation Front. Why didn't you do it? You know from now on you are prisoners, Angkar's prisoners; in principle we should shoot you, but there are so many of you and the ammunition is too expensive ... So Angkar is going to make a selection to eliminate the bad elements by work and hardship. Angkar needs a new people, pure and hard-working. Everybody will become *kamakors* (peasants) and *kaksekors* (workers). There'll be no more schools, no more books; your university will be the forest and the paddy fields; you'll earn your diplomas with your tears and the sweat of your brow. Your money, that of the imperialist Lon Nol, isn't worth anything any more, it'll be replaced by Angkar's new money.[2] In any case you won't have any; you'll live by the fruit of your labours, by barter, and by what Angkar gives to you.

Listen, Comrades! Abandon any hope of going back to your homes in Phnom Penh! Your city has become a vast storehouse. There are no more embassies, no more Americans, no more French ... the country no longer needs foreign aid! From now on western medicine will be replaced by herbs ... We've no further need for fuel oils, as the machines will run on charcoal. The French, when they left our country, left their cars, and we thank them! But we'll use our legs and we'll salvage the motors for agricultural machinery or for canoes, while the tyres will be good for making sandals ...

I think of our beautiful car that Seng had entrusted to Mr Thiên, believing that it would be looked after safely, all the while proving of invaluable service to Angkar ... The speech continues. I ask myself if I'm not in the middle of a terrible nightmare – in the cause of progress, Cambodia is going backwards! I begin to despair, but my husband, inveterate optimist as ever, always so confident in the regime, begins to reassure me: "Angkar's right. This way we can create a strong and pure nation," and he murmurs in my ear: "We must *to sou*."[3]

2. In fact they pin up some new money, which will never be used, at the entrance to the pagoda.
3. A Cambodian term meaning "to struggle" and used in one of the main propaganda slogans of the time; *to sou pakdevat*; one must 'struggle to make the revolution.' ...

At the end of the first harangue, another man starts speaking: "Angkar will need a workforce, especially factory workers in Phnom Penh, as it is going to reopen the weaving factories, the factories for batteries, fishing nets and also for condensed milk, like Sokilait … "

I wake up when I hear the name because I was the executive secretary at Sokilait.

The Khmer Rouge soldier continues: "Right now you must tell us exactly who you are, and the exact truth about your past, and your skills. Don't hide anything from Angkar, who has to make a choice."

Everyone then receives a questionnaire to fill out, on which you must state your surname, first name, profession under the old regime and the number of people in your family. Most Cambodians understand the tactic, which is to single out soldiers, teachers or doctors – in a word all the intellectuals – who are considered traitors. Everyone declares they are peasants, street vendors, coolies, street sweepers or bicycle-rickshaw drivers … Everyone, or nearly everyone, with the exception of Seng, who above all believes that one mustn't lie to Angkar, and who gives precise information on his whole family: I'm French. I work at the French Embassy. He is a self-employed businessman, who has done a lot of work for military officials. In short, he proudly confesses all that should have been concealed.

Once all the papers have been gathered in, Angkar declares the meeting over. Now we're allowed to eat the contents of our mess tins in a suddenly relaxed and celebratory atmosphere. Each of us can already imagine returning to Phnom Penh and we rejoice, even if it means working there as a labourer. For a fleeting moment, I imagine myself back working at Sokilait. I'll tell Angkar that I know the factory and that I once worked there; it's a little daydream that helps me forget our appalling situation for a few minutes.

Back on the island at the end of the afternoon, the village chief calls us together, as he does every evening after work; we must be well educated … He announces to us that, from now on, it is formally forbidden to speak anything other than Khmer. I, who haven't yet mastered the language, will have to keep quiet as I learn on the job. As night falls, Mr Thiên also advises us not to reminisce, as Angkar doesn't like the spirit to be led astray by the life of corruption that we used to know. But for the moment, we haven't got into this habit, as we have neither the inclination nor the time to upset ourselves with yesterday's pleasures. The memories will come later, when we are truly hungry; during our work in the fields, my sister-in-law and I will reminisce in lowered tones about our favourite foods, and our surreal whispers will make us drool.

But the chief has spoken. We are not allowed to talk about the past.

As far as the future is concerned, it seems truly dark.

According to Angkar's commandments, each village is ordered to house between fifty and a hundred families. On the island, Mr Thiên continues to take in refugees; five to ten families arrive every day, always the well off, all the more profitable to shake down.

Days, weeks, months pass. How many? We no longer have a calendar. Since our arrival, I have tried to keep a sense of time by writing the date on the wall of our straw hut with a piece of charcoal.

There's still no news about our return to Phnom Penh. My life as a peasant goes on; a life without electricity, without running water; rising daily at five in the morning, a quick wash in the river, then, on an empty stomach, it's off to the cornfields, to the sugar cane or to the tobacco fields, to water, weed or to plant manioc, sweet potatoes, peanuts and a variety of vegetables – marrow, pumpkins, cucumbers, beans and aubergines. I learn to plant tobacco, an extremely precious and sought-after commodity. The island produces it to exchange for the palm sugar it lacks. Tobacco production is paramount and requires a lot of work; gathering, drying and cutting. Then there is the cultivation of rice which is of fundamental importance. For this I must learn to turn over the earth, sow, weed, transplant, harvest and thresh the stalks to get the grain and then pound it to obtain the totally white rice. There's no time for idling. When the land on the island runs out, the inhabitants work the mainland, to the west, where there are several hectares of paddy fields to which we are sent – men, women and children

I learn to work the earth.

Bit by bit, I learn how to deal with my gaolers, how to navigate in their troubled waters and how to play at being submissive to escape death. Because of my French nationality, the converted Khmer peasants and the Khmer Rouge, particularly their women, make fun of me viciously and call me *yé barang* (old French woman) or *yé ponso* (old *ponso* – it's a corruption of my family name, which Cambodians can't pronounce):

"So, *yé barang*, in your country, would you work like this?"

"Oh no, comrade!"

"Are you happy to be here?"

"Yes, comrade! Thanks to Angkar I've learned lots of new things. In my country, I would never have learned all this. Yes, yes, I'm very happy to do what I do here because otherwise I'd have never known any of it."

It is what they want to hear and I gibber it at them – in Khmer, of course.

I bend in the direction of the wind, like the reeds.

After a month, the food really begins to run out. Besides rice, corn and salt, we have nothing left. We collect fallen mangoes and rotten papayas that have been half eaten by birds. Sometimes we manage to exchange a few aspirins for some duck eggs. As far as meat and fish are concerned, it's up to us to be wily enough to get hold of them ourselves.

At the age of thirty-one, I've suddenly become an old woman. I'm completely dried up. In the first few months, with the emotional trauma and the enforced diet, my periods disappear – they will only return a year after my liberation by the Vietnamese. It's the same for my sister-in-law Li, my nieces, and all the other refugees. Only the wives of the Khmer Rouge or the affluent villagers who tow the party line keep a regular cycle, because they eat normally … But, since it seems we live in paradise, we've no right to complain.

The workers are divided into categories and food is allocated according to what they produce. At the top of the ladder are the men and young people, who are considered the premier workforce (*yuvachuon*); then the women in good health (*yutneary*), who have just about enough strength to get by. At the bottom are the old people, the young children and the sick adults, be it physically or psychologically – those who do not have the will to work and are considered 'useless mouths'. They must make do with a meagre portion, when they are not completely deprived of their daily rations and forced to take some from other family members.

My ten-year-old son, Jean-Jacques, works. He receives an adult ration; his sister Jeannie, who is only seven-years-old, is not productive; she is entitled to only half that amount. That's equality under the regime.

Ultimately, for the Khmer Rouge, old people and the sick count for nothing; they are useless.

Each group of workers is under the control of someone who is also a *schlop*. But there is really no need for the *yauth-eas* to keep watch over us; where could we run away to? We are registered here, how could we find food elsewhere? How can you revolt without weapons, and when the men are taken away, one after the other? The refugees are passive, exhausted by the first few weeks; physically and mentally, resistance basically consists of staying alive.

We work five or six days in a row, then we are given a free morning to go fishing … well, that is, if you know how to do it!

One day, I manage to go on a fishing trip with some women from the village. Another new experience for a townie like me. We set off in a canoe at five in the morning for the island of Taloun, east of Tukveal. There, at low tide, a sort of marshland called *bengs* is revealed, where the fish dig themselves into the mud to lay their eggs. We wade out into the water up to our knees. The fishing is done with an open wicker fish trap that is placed on the top of the water.

You stir the mud to flush out the fish and then catch them in the trap. For me it is a difficult and athletic task but, for the villagers, it's child's play … In one day, with their help, I manage to catch several kilos of all sorts of fish, including a water snake, which with its highly-prized flesh is enough to feed the whole family for a few days.

After that, my sister-in-law finds another miraculous way of fishing, from which I benefit. Freshwater fish like to eat human excrement; armed with this biological fact, we get up very early in the morning, before everyone else, and go down to the riverbank and onto a small low pontoon. We put a wicker basket in the water, holding it with two hands, then we do our morning business into it; immediately we hear the fish wriggling in the basket, which we quickly pull out. This way we catch five or six fish every time.

It's System D, a temporary solution to help us and our children survive.

I get on very well with Li. She's a kind, brave, hard-working woman like all Chinese, and her zen-like composure in the face of our hardship still astonishes me. Her blind faith in the regime probably allows her to distance herself from our reality. Thank goodness she's here with me. Although we are not allowed to express ourselves or recall our past, we keep each other's morale up and understand each other instinctively.

I can't quite remember now how we all felt at the time. How do Jean-Jacques, Jeannie and the nieces and nephews react to the situation? What do the little ones do all day, while we're in the fields? They're no longer allowed to play with their dolls, play hopscotch or hide and seek, or to skip like all other children of their age; they no longer go to school and never have enough to eat. I only remember that they snivel every morning before our departure and beg for a breakfast which never arrives. Then, having no more energy to ask any questions, they look vacant, they're silent – it's clear they understand the situation. It's as if, despite their presence, they're absent. They never ask: "Maman, Papa, what's going on, what are we going to do?" For our part, we no longer kiss or cuddle them as we once did. For fear of reprisals, I no longer have fun with Jeannie nor lavish any attention on her. All the little daily gestures that create intimacy between parents and children no longer exist. Everything between us is wiped out. The children look after themselves; they wash alone in the river and eat the first meal of the day, which Angkar hands out at noon, alone. Today, thinking back on it, I suffer terribly.

At first, when I realise that they aren't going to school anymore, that they aren't learning anything, I ask myself in anguish how they are ever going to catch up. Then I bitterly regret not having entrusted them to Michel Deverge, the Cultural Attaché. But little by little, my preoccupation with my own stomach takes my mind off these things ... We're caught in a hellish chain, a mortal trap, which closes in on us a little bit more day by day. We have to work, work harder and harder for our own and our children's survival.

While I'm sent with Li to the manioc or sweet potato fields, my husband clears the forest with the men. I don't see him during the day; he leaves at dawn with his wicker mess tin and comes back only at nightfall. As always, he remains chatty ...

Seng creates what he believes is a mutual bond of friendship with Mr Thiên. At no moment does he have any doubts about him, and not for one second does he suspect that this man spies for Angkar and is looking for traitors to expose, as the Khmer Rouge's purification is not only ethnic but social. Seng doesn't know that he is already on the list of people 'to be eliminated', he still knows nothing …

When we are short of rice, Mr Thiên steps in. When Mr Thiên falls ill, my husband ransacks our precious medical supplies to give him aspirins. One day, when he's on his way back from a field on the mainland, my husband meets two friends at the pagoda who have just arrived with their families. It's the former landlord of our apartment in Phnom Penh. He's a police chief; his son is a soldier of the former government, and there's another neighbour, a school teacher. Seng decides to ask the village chief if they can be housed next to us. He accepts our request straight away. Believing he is doing the right thing, Seng reveals the identity and profession of his 'comrades'. But, without realising it, he has just committed a monumental error – he has signed their death warrants, and his own.

Seng talks far too much. At every chance he tells Mr Thiên how much he admires Angkar's work, eulogises the Chinese communists, and proclaims the thoughts of Mao. He also becomes friends with a hunchback dwarf in the village, to whom he spouts his political convictions. He tells him that he listens to *Radio Peking* on the little portable radio we've managed to salvage. According to the Chinese, Samdech Sihanouk will return to Phnom Penh and the whole population will go back to the capital and pick up their lives as before. What a gaffe! The hunchback dwarf turns out to be a *schlop*! One night around midnight, some *yautheas* gather silently at Mr Thiên's for a secret meeting. We live next door. I'm worrying about our situation, and I can't get to sleep. I strain my ear to try to understand what they are saying and catch some snippets of the conversation. "Don't let the newcomers listen to foreign radio stations," they say, "Confiscate the radios," and also: "Repatriate the Vietnamese!" Even though I don't speak Khmer very well, I understand perfectly what they are saying. Deeply uneasy, I wake Seng to tell him what I've heard, but he rebuffs me, saying that I've probably not understood, and anyway there is nothing to fear.

The next day, Mr Thiên asks my husband to tune his radio into the national network; the day after that he borrows it, pretending his is broken. We never see it again. But my husband still cannot understand that silence is golden. On the way to the fields, he continues to discuss big ideas with his friend the police chief, telling him what he's managed to glean from here and there. Soon they're spotted by the *schlops* and followed closely. At this point the hunchback dwarf begins to ask Jean-Jacques questions: "Does your dad have gun? Have you ever seen him in military uniform?" This interrogation really worries me, but Seng is unaffected and tries to reassure me.

The police chief doesn't bring Seng any luck. A big-mouth, he shows off a lot, flouts the rules, and continues to speak French and English. Two months after his arrival, four *schlops* take him away one evening after supper. They claim that Angkar needs his help. He is the first 'admission' – as the villagers on the island say – to a re-education camp.[4]

---

4. To be admitted to a 're-education camp' meant to be condemned to death, but nobody knew this at this point, except for the Khmer Rouge and their families.

About two weeks after his arrest, on 15 July 1975, the *schlops* return at five in the morning and take twenty other men before they leave for work. Among them are the police chief's son, the former Lon Nol soldier, the schoolmaster, who was our neighbour in Phnom Penh, and Seng. The spies lie to the children: "Don't worry; your father will come back. Angkar is taking him to an education camp to *rieng-soth* (to learn)."

The same day, at four o'clock in the morning, I had been sent off with the other women to the cornfields on the west of the island. When I get back in the evening, I find the children in tears in front of the hut. I ask them what is going on. Mr Thiên intervenes, trying to reassure me: "Angkar only wants to get some information because your husband was denounced by his friend the police chief, but he'll be back in twenty-four, forty-eight hours at most. Don't worry!"

And that was the last we ever heard of Seng.

If it weren't for my sister-in-law, Li, I'd feel completely and utterly alone.

Every evening after work, I see naked corpses tied to the trunks of banana trees, floating past my hut by the river's edge. Secretly, I pray to God that my husband's body isn't among them.

The month of July sees the first harvest of corn on the mainland. In a single day, the team of women must harvest two to three hectares of corn cobs, load them onto carts and carry them to the river's edge where then they must be loaded onto the canoes. In the evening, on returning to the island, they dish out around twenty kilos per person from the harvest, to last the whole season. As a result, we receive less rice and from now on only eat corn in various forms, morning and evening. This monotonous diet unsettles our bowels.

Two weeks after the arrest of the 'traitors', Angkar requisitions our 'home', the makeshift hut, a second time. That very day we are made to leave the island at three in the morning to work in a field seven kilometres from the village. When we get back, the children tell us that Mr Thiên came with two *schlops* and searched our bags. Evidently, these spies, who skulk around the houses at night, eavesdropping on our conversations, should be avoided like the plague. But no one ever knows who is a *schlop* … The first time they did a search, I'd managed to hide a few things, but this time almost everything has been stolen, everything that the Khmer Rouge have judged unnecessary for us but highly useful for them – medicine, soap … as well as my precious address book. For me the loss of this little book symbolises a total and final break with my 'corrupt' life.

Towards the end of August, a rumour goes round that Angkar is going to allow the population to be reintroduced back into the towns or provinces that they came from. As though to confirm this piece of news, boats set off down the Mekong and return loaded with refugees. Nobody knows where they will disembark. Some say Phnom Penh, others Kompong Chhnang … leaflets are distributed in the villages, asking those originating in the provinces of Kompong Cham, Kompong Chhnang, Kompong Thom, Svay Rieng and Prey Veng to return home. What a joy! Everyone wants to leave immediately except the Phnompenhois, who haven't received authorisation to return to the capital. As a last formality before leaving the place, the *moulakhans* (island-ers) claim that Angkar has to confiscate a few more of our goods.

Once again, the refugees are tricked by the infamous Angkar; no repatriation whatsoever takes place into the provinces they came from. Instead there is a second depor-tation into regions that are even more wretched and even more hostile, and where even more barbaric conditions await them.

Towards the middle of September, Mr Thiên receives a list of all the families who have ever lived in Phnom Penh; my sister-in-law and I must leave the island with our chil-dren that very day. I'm not at all enthusiastic, because I still hope – largely encouraged by the village chief - that one day Seng will come back. I'm told: "Don't worry, set your mind at rest, your husband will know where to find you…" This doesn't really reassure me, especially as Mr Thiên's mother strongly advises me against going. "My poor girl, you aren't going to Phnom Penh – the town is reserved for the families of the *yautheas*. You're going into the mountains where there is nothing. Try to get authorisation to stay with us. I love you as a daughter and we need people like you, willing workers." I ask her to plead our case to her son. It's in vain – the list comes from on high; the order is irreversible.

We leave Mr Thiên's mother with the things that will weigh us down like the coloured clothes that we can't wear and the pots and pans, but we do keep one saucepan and a kettle. On 15 September 1975, five months after our arrival and two months after Seng's disappearance, we leave the island with heavy hearts.

In the early afternoon, a canoe drops Li, the children and

I off on the mainland, at the pagoda, which is already full with those hoping to return home. In the evening, Mr Thiên comes for the last time to hand out our rice ration. Li and I light a fire to cook it; with no wood to burn, we reluctantly use the banknotes of the old regime as fuel. The two million riels do their job well …

Gradually, for no reason at all, hope overcomes fear. We are so excited that we have trouble sleeping that night.

5/ The Voyage of No Return

What a surprise it is the following morning, to see a convoy of military trucks! Everyone is happy and excited, impatient to set off. We all think that Phnom Penh awaits us.

At registration, I once more calmly and confidently give my name, first name, and the number of people in my family. Once this formality is over, there's a new search, a new confiscation and we watch in despair as the few possessions we have left vanish into thin air. Then one of the *yautheas* grabs my photo album and hurls it violently to the ground, saying bluntly: "No souvenirs to remember your past life. All must be wiped out and forgotten." I cry, I implore him, I tell him that this is all that I have left of my parents, of my father. He looks at the photo of Papa, covered in decorations awarded by the King of Cambodia … hesitates for a second … and then says dryly: "Okay, comrade, you can keep this photo, but only this one", and throws out all the others, although my nieces manage to collect them and they disappear into their pockets.

Then we all set off, herded like animals into lorries bearing the hallmark 'Made in China'.[1] The tarpaulins are lowered. We get going around nine – I don't have a watch anymore

---

1. It's strange that these lorries should be 'Made in China', since during the first welcome speech in the pagoda Angkar had told us that the country had no need for any foreign aid.

but I guess what time it is from the position of the sun. We follow the journey through slits in the tarpaulin. After Takhmau, instead of going straight southwards to Phnom Penh, the lorry makes a long detour westwards via Kompong Kantuot, and follows the Pochentong road into town. We're all mad with joy when we glimpse the first houses as we still believe that we are going to be resettled in the capital.

The trucks enter a deserted town. With the exception of a few *yautheas* all dressed in black, on foot or on bicycles, there's not a soul to be seen. We cross Phnom Penh, passing in front of the central market; it's completely empty, but surrounded by magnificent coconut trees. I wonder how 'they' have managed to grow such beautiful coconut-laden palms in such a short time. In fact, I will learn later that, under each tree, they have buried those killed in the summary executions that took place immediately after the fall of Phnom Penh. The monsters!

Then our lorry heads towards the north of town where we think they are going to settle us. As we drive along the Boulevard Monivong leading to the French Embassy, my heart beats wildly at the sight of this street that's so familiar to me. It leaves me feeling sad and deeply moved. To the left, in front of the embassy, the cathedral has been turned into a pile of stones; to the right, the grand Hotel Royal is still standing, as is the Lycée Descartes where I went to school; a little further away, the embassy residences are still there, but they're deserted and in front of them a cornfield is sprouting. They don't waste any time — the slogan is "every plot of land must be cultivated"; they want to annihilate everything linked to capitalism and to take everyone back to an agricultural life.

But still we don't stop, and all the houses are empty. Further on, when I catch a glimpse of Sokilait, the condensed milk factory, I shake all over and recall with anger the *yautheas* speeches at the first meeting in the pagoda when we were told Angkar needed us for the factories; a lie to make us reveal our backgrounds ... Besides the *yautheas*, there is absolutely no trace of life in Phnom Penh. We leave the northern quarter and continue by the main road; I realise that the Khmer Rouge have tricked us once more, and that we'll never see our houses again.

It must be one or two o'clock in the afternoon, as the sun has begun to go down. We've been driving since the morning without a single break for the toilet. The old people, the sick and the children are no longer able to hold it in and do it in the lorry. A nauseating smell starts to envelop us, but the *yautheas* don't care and act as if they're transporting beasts, not human beings. In total despair, everyone begins to cry out, to rant and rave, demanding a stop, which is granted at last. We pour out of the lorry to relieve ourselves and to breathe a bit of fresh air. In our lorry, two old people have died. We are all hungry and thirsty, but there isn't much left in our baskets — just a little bit of cold rice, some salt and dregs of boiled water in a gourd that will do for the children, who cry with hunger but still don't ask a single question. They are content simply to eat if there is still something left to eat, en route to their tragic destiny ...

After a few minutes, we have to get back into the tarpaulin-covered cattle truck; we cram in, pushing the corpses to the side, as they will be continuing their journey with us. Someone dares to ask: "*Mith*, where are we going?" Curtly, the *yauthea* next to the driver answers: "We aren't there yet".

All the towns of the province we pass through turn out to be as deserted as Phnom Penh. The journey seems to go on forever — night fell a long time ago and the children are dead tired but, consumed by hunger, they can't sleep and start whining again. We're still driving without knowing our final destination and our tormenters make absolutely no effort to find out if we need any food or water.

At last, around midnight, we arrive at our first stop, Pursat. Apparently we're to catch a train from here tomorrow. The place is seething with a crowd of refugees just like us. The *yautheas* show us the place where rice and salt will be handed out and everyone makes a mad dash for it. After a long wait, Li and I get hold of some priceless supplies, but we still have to find somewhere to set up a tent and shelter from the damp. The children, worn out and starving, cry non-stop. The night is dark, there's no moon, and I feel ill at ease ... Since being plunged brutally back into the Middle Ages, I bless the nights when the full moon gives us light. I ask a woman where I can find some water to boil the rice. She points out a pool on the outskirts of the camp, around which some silhouettes are circulating, cloaked in darkness. So blindly, with only two thoughts in my head, to drink and to cook the rice, I plunge a bucket into the vaguely whitish water ... With some hastily-gathered stones my sister-in-law and I manage to set up a sort of hearth. Once the hunger of the grownups and the little small ones is more or less satisfied, we roll out the mats on the ground, hang up the mosquito nets as best we can on the four branches which we have managed to gather together, and go to sleep hoping that tomorrow will be better.

At dawn, I go back to the pool to freshen up. I heave

violently when I see the sight; surrounding the pool are piles of human excrement. It's clear the whole camp has to come here to relieve themselves — it's disgusting, but whether it be clear or polluted, water is essential and this is all there is in the camp.

We spend three days in these conditions; we're given rice, salt and a little palm sugar and we use the stagnant water for cooking. There's nothing to do, nothing to see; stuck in open country, near the town of Pursat alongside the railway line, we sit and wait. If the calendar I keep in my head is right, the train that's expected to arrive the following day only turns up on 19 September 1975, at about five in the afternoon. It's an empty goods train. We receive orders to board immediately. The designated families (of which we are one) dash up, hurling their meagre bundles of possessions willy-nilly into the corners of the wagon. In turn, we take our place. There are no seats; each person has just enough room to sit on the floor. Once everyone is crammed into the wagon these monsters announce, without giving any reason, that the train isn't leaving and we must spend the night in it. The wagon is full to bursting point; sitting, legs crossed, squashed up one against the other, we try to sleep in vain. I take my little daughter in my arms to help her nod off in a position that's a little more comfortable. Li does the same with Ha. Jean-Jacques stretches out as best he can, his head resting on my folded legs. I don't sleep a wink all night; my legs are full of pins and needles. At six in the morning, an ear-splitting siren wakes us up and a *yauthea* passes by announcing that the train is about to leave. We've just enough time to jump out to go to the toilet before the clanking wagons set off. Jolted awake, the children start to cry and clamour for food. At every meal, we somehow manage to save a little cold rice with some salt to take the edge off their hunger. Li and I do without. For ten hours we trundle on without stopping. As before, some old people relieve themselves on the spot. Stuffed in this over-crowded, stinking wagon, my distress reaches breaking point as the hours pass. To kill the time, which seems like an eternity, I look out of the wagon's poky window and from time to time I can make out the names of the stations we pass. They haven't yet had time to Khmerise the names, they're still in French: Battambang, Svay Chet, Samrong, Mongkolborey. At last, around four o'clock in the afternoon, we arrive at our second stop, Svay Sisophon, another provincial town.

Svay Sisophon seethes with refugees from other provinces. Outside the station the *yautheas* are getting organised; they put the families in groups of ten (*krums*); every *krum* is supervised by a chief. Once more we have to fill in forms with our names, first names and the number of people in our family, and give them to the chiefs who give each *krum* a number. My sister-in-law, her children, my children and I are all registered as a single family although we are in fact two; this unfair grouping will constantly penalise us when rations are distributed. We belong to *krum* No. 62.

With the completed forms, each *krum* leader can get rice and salted dried fish from the *yautheas*. When the formalities are over, we are ordered to go to the centre of town where a wooden hut is allocated to each family for the night.

We spend twenty-four hours at Svay Sisophon, not knowing what will happen next. This uncertainty saps our morale, but we must wait. There's nothing to do to pass the time — no music, no books, just total emptiness. We sit glaring at each other, unable even to laugh or joke with the children, who in any case have no desire to — they're unhappy, starving, and listless. For nearly six months now, without understanding, they've submitted to their sad fate. Deep despair is written across their faces, but they neither want nor dare to ask us questions.

At dawn on 22 September, some tractors come to collect us to take us to a new destination. I'd never travelled and moved about so much in my life and this was only just the beginning. Each tractor loads up two *krums*, that's twenty families; we are mere livestock pulled along according to the whims of Angkar, we are at Angkar's mercy, we have become its property. Angkar can do with our lives what it wishes. And bizarrely, not one of us has the idea, the wish or the will to revolt, fearing reprisal and lacking the means ...

After two hours, we arrive in a mountainous region sur-rounded by three *phnoms*: Phnom Leap, Phnom Trayon, Phnom Traloch.[2] The tractors unload their human cargo in the hospital courtyard of Phnom Leap where some oxcarts are waiting for us; once again our possessions are hurled willy-nilly into the carts. We follow on foot, barefoot, under a blazing sun — it must be around eleven in the morning — until we get to a pagoda that's about three kilometres away. The thirsty, starving and exhausted children drag wea-rily behind the cortèges, snivelling. Heartbroken, we don't know what to do to console or comfort them. It's shocking that, in a country so abundant with fruit trees, it's months

---

2. Phnom means 'hill'. Each *phnom* can be no higher than six hundred metres.

since we saw a banana, a mango or an orange. To stop them getting worn out by the walk, I carry Jeannie on my back and Li does the same with Ha. In front of the pagoda, three village chiefs are waiting for us at the bottom of Phnom Traloch: Ta Chen, Ta Svay and Ta Krach.[3] Picked at random with fourteen other families, we are selected by Ta Chen, the leader of the poorest village, where the people are greedy and envious. It seems that bad luck is following us ... Once the allocation is finished, we have to march behind the carts for another three kilometres to our new place of detention, which is more terrible than the last, but better than that which is yet to come.

---

3. *Ta* is the title given to a man. The term *louk* for 'Mr' under the old regime is banned from the vocabulary.

6/ The Second 'Residence'

Our adoptive village is evenly divided into *krums*. There are five of them, each headed by a chief. My sister-in-law and I are placed in *krum* No. 2, whose chief is called Pouk Sem.[1]

The villagers immediately set themselves apart from the refugees, whom they call *neak thmey* (new inhabitants); they are the *neak chak* (old inhabitants). Each of the old families has to take in two or three of the new families according to the size of their straw hut. We are parachuted onto a young mother with two children, who is nice but rather nosy. Her husband works in Chuop and only comes back to see his family now and again.

Once Pouk Sem has introduced us, our 'hostess' shows us our allotted space. There is no electricity, certainly not in a backwater like this, and no river either, so there's not as much water as there was in Tukveal. At the edge of the village there are some muddy ponds where men and animals come to quench their thirst. Behind the hut there is a place set aside for our needs; you must dig a hole every time you go which you then cover up — dead leaves make do as toilet paper.

We settle in; Pouk Sem hands out rice and salt for supper.

---

1. *Pouk* means father or papa. In this region this is the name given to men of a certain age who are owed respect. The term *Mè* is used for the wife of a *Pouk* or of all ladies older than us.

The very next day, we are called to a brainwashing session where we hear the usual speech, the same recommendations and the same prohibitions. We must only speak Khmer; no talking in the evening, as Angkar has ears everywhere; we mustn't wear glasses, the sign of being an intellectual. When we arrived the day before, a *yauthea* approached a short-sighted man in our group and asked him brutally: "Do you really need to see so far? No!" Then he ripped his glasses off, threw them on the ground and stamped on them, saying scornfully: "From now on you won't need these to see clearly … "

We have to work to earn our daily rice ration. We are still only allowed two meals a day, and we can't eat proper rice grains either, only rice soup, because this is a very poor area. We also get a few salted dried fish; there are no fruit or vegetables.

Disciplining our children is absolutely forbidden, as from now on they are 'Angkar's children'. Just after our arrival in the village, I was taken to task on this very point. One evening, tired and exhausted by the hardship, I couldn't stand poor Jeannie's incessant crying any longer. Overwhelmed with hunger, I lost patience and smacked her, which, instead of calming her down, made her cry even more. A *schlop* saw me and, in front of my sobbing daughter, reminded me severely that I no longer had the right to lay a hand on her.

So there is the distribution of orders and the prohibitions. Strange as it may seem, Angkar continues to promise us a better life. Very soon, we'll see, we'll be rewarded. Foolishly, we all live in hope …

After our first re-education meeting, Pouk Sem visits each family to compile a sort of curriculum vitae, where we must tell the truth, the whole truth, and nothing but the truth. The sorting out continues ... Scrupulously following my absent husband's advice to be honest (at this moment Seng is still alive for me), I declare that before 17 April 1975, I was a secretary at the French Embassy ... which immediately provokes the scorn of our petty chief, who replies sarcastically: "Understand that from now on Angkar doesn't need bureaucrats, only *kamakors* and *kaksekors*."

As soon as the administrative formalities are completed, to our horrified disbelief and immense dismay, Pouk Sem orders Li's three daughters, Leng, Hoa and Phan, as well as my son Jean-Jacques, to pick up their personal belongings – he is taking them to work far from the village. Angkar urgently needs workers for the construction of dykes (*tonoups*) in Chuop, Svay Sisophon and Taphon. As young people are considered the principal workforce, boys and girls from ten years of age are conscripted first ... Pouk Sem assures us that our children will be well-fed and well-treated. But the poor little things will only be entitled to the same pittance as us and will be forced to work fifteen hours a day.

Bereft and taken completely by surprise, Li and I begin to cry. Pouk Sem brutally brings us back to order — tears are forbidden, no matter what the circumstance. This is neither more nor less than an order from Angkar, and all orders coming from Angkar Leu (from on high) are irrevocable. With a heavy heart, we watch our children leave, asking ourselves what awaits them.

Yet there's no time to worry about what will become of them. We are too preoccupied with the two little ones, Jeannie and Ha, and the daily struggle against exhaustion and the hunger which gnaws away at us night and day and the sickness which has just began to rear its head …

Every day in the village there are a thousand chores waiting for us; weeding the potato, corn and manioc fields, making bundles of sugar palm leaves to thatch the roofs of the huts, and clearing the forest … We leave for work as the cock crows, with a bowl of water and a grain of salt in our stomachs. The salt gives the sensation of being full up but it doesn't give any nourishment. They give us rough grain salt that is black and unrefined; even so you have to hide it or it'll disappear. When hunger wakes me up in the middle of the night, I suck a grain of salt, pretending it's a sweet, and drink a large bowl of water. It gives the illusion of having had a light meal. At midday and in the evening, we gulp down a bowl of rice soup. On the odd lucky day you might see a lump or two of manioc floating in each ladle, but most of the time it is an insipid liquid from which it's difficult to fish out even a spoonful of rice.

We suffer both physically and mentally. Powerless, we watch the children wasting away before our eyes.

Deliberately, Angkar has made no effort to supply these far-flung camps; we suffer daily from the ensuing cruel shortages. We are all destined for certain death. We supplement our meals with what we can harvest locally; leaves from sweet potatoes and manioc, bamboo shoots, wild spinach full of spikes, and *kapok* shoots.[2] When we arrived, there were toads swarming all over the village. When I catch one during the day, I put it in my pocket which I tie up carefully to stop it escaping. I can feel the poor beast stuck in the dark blow up and pee … In the evening, I take it out of its prison, and - whack! - in one fell swoop, I chop off its head. Soon I

---

2. *Kapok* is a sort of cotton whose fruit, before flowering, is edible.

can't hear any toads croaking around the village anymore — we've eaten them all before they have had time to breed.

In principle, the food ration is divided equally among us, but it's a fixed rate for each family. When we registered, Pouk Sem put Li and I together as one family, so we always lose out on the food supplies. For example, we only get one ration of dried fish, manioc or sweet potatoes instead of two. As for the rice, it is doled out to each person every day; but it's unfairly distributed; the original residents get twice as much as the newcomers and, as though by a miracle, during the weeks of shortage they always have some reserves and tell us that we don't know how to economise.

And this is the way it will always be; when we eat one bowl of solid rice, the old residents eat twice as much. When we are on a diet of salted rice soup, the villagers and the *yautheas* feed themselves on proper whole rice, fish soups, sweet potatoes, bananas, palm sugar ...

If we want more to eat, we have to barter the few precious things we still have left. Thank goodness we left Phnom Penh loaded up like pack horses! At each stage the Khmer Rouge relieve us of a little bit more; after a few months we will have nothing left but a blanket, a mosquito net (very valuable), and the strict minimum of clothes and crockery .... but there won't be a single piece of jewellery left to barter, so the hardship lying ahead of us will be all the more harsh and painful.

In November, the first rice harvest, which was planted before our arrival in the village, begins. All the women are conscripted. It's a tough apprenticeship. At Koh Tukveal I worked in the corn, manioc and sweet potato fields and at drying tobacco leaves, but not in the paddy fields. I have never held a sickle in my life, so during the first week I regularly cut the fingers on my left hand. When all five are covered in cuts, it means the lesson has begun to sink in.

But the most disgusting test is the leeches; in all the Cambodian paddy fields you find little fish, crabs, snails, and also leeches. These horrible beasts immediately latch on to your feet, your legs and even your private parts without you realising. They don't let go or fall off until they have gorged themselves with blood. It's grisly!

The first time I'm sent to harvest a flooded rice paddy, I can't bear to step into the water. At once one of those vile *schlops* turns up and brutally orders me to obey: "Look, old Frenchy, if you don't go in, you'll get no ration this evening. And it's the same for all of you who refuse to go into paddy fields infested with leeches!"

Seeing my distress, an old villager gives me some tips to stop them getting onto my body: "Roll your trousers up to the knee, then tie rushes round them; this way the creatures will attach themselves to your wrists or your calves, but no further up." I follow her advice and step into the paddy field with my eyes shut; the call of my stomach is stronger than anything. I think of my rice ration, which is priceless to me and my daughter … Despite all this, it's absolutely disgusting to get out with these greeny-black suckers glued onto my wrists and legs. They only fall off if you heat them up, with a cigarette butt, for example; but since cigarettes have become almost impossible to find, I content myself with prising them off with the sickle.

During the harvest, from November 1975 to January 1976,

life seems to get a little bit sweeter. Once or twice a month Pouk Sem gives us one or two little pieces of palm sugar which I carefully put aside for Jeannie, who is starting to get seriously anaemic. Every day I see that she's weaker and more unhappy; she's wasting away. She doesn't work, and still only gets a half-ration, so I continue to go without so she can have more. Luckily, we all get double rations for the three months of the harvest: two helpings of rice a day for us, the newcomers, and four for the villagers, according to the famous egalitarian principles of the communist regime!

While I'm out harvesting, Li volunteers to thresh the paddy (unthreshed) rice. It is an extremely tiring job but, at the end of the day, she gets some of the rice bran which the Khmer Rouge keep to feed the pigs. We regard this as a right royal supplement, as it gives more bulk to our meals. More importantly, rice bran is full of vitamins, and it is probably due to this substitute that I survived the Pol Pot regime without losing either my teeth or my hair. Alas, each 'pleasure' has its price — it messes up our intestines and we suffer constant diarrhoea.

When I was an 'intellectual', I didn't know that rice had to be threshed to get the grains out. So the first time there is a shortage in the village and they give us paddy rice, I just cook it as usual, in a saucepan with water. Two hours, and lots of firewood later, the paddy is still in one piece. Not understanding what's gone wrong, I ask the villager we live with who makes fun of me, viciously: "Look at these towns-folk; until today they've eaten rice, lots of rice, never asking themselves how it gets onto their plates." All the same she explains to me how to pound it with a pestle to get the grain out without damaging it too much, and to put it all in a type of wicker basket that works as a sieve and removes the husk from the grain, and then the bran from the rice itself. It was fortunate that she showed me how to do this as at the next place we're assigned we are never given any rice, and when we manage to steal some paddy from the fields we'll have to sort it out ourselves.

Brutally wrenched from our daily comforts and tossed overnight into country life, we'll learn a thousand different things. For example, if you put crabs in with minnows they'll eat them up. That's how one day, I cried 'thief' when there were only crabs left in my bowl. I had put them in there with the minnows I had collected that morning while planting out in the paddy fields .. .

Threshing starts at five in the morning. Each *krum* has three pestles. By eleven it's done. We only thresh twenty sacks of paddy a day for five *krums* (fifty families).

Outside working hours, harvesting or threshing, we can go fishing. Although fishing is a big word — it would be more accurate to say foraging for small fry in the paddy fields with a two-handled wicker basket. We scrape the bottom of the fields flooded forty to fifty centimetres deep, lift the basket from which the water drains out and sort what is left on the bottom: tadpoles, little freshwater crabs, small fish, snails, sometimes little water-snakes and always more leeches. Leaving those aside, the rest can all be eaten; the smallest shrimp is a source of protein. It's not the moment to be picky about taste. Hunger gnaws away at us, and we'll eat anything. Beef and pork are extremely rare; we will only get them on important occasions, like the Khmer Rouge victory feast in April. We'll even end up eating rotten meat crawling with maggots. One day, they kill two sick cows which they then bury. A few days later, I go with two other women and dig them up. They're already badly decomposed — the meat is green, bitter and crawling with maggots — but we're desperate to eat. When there's no more fish or edible water plants, there are still the cockroaches. Our hut is swarming with them, and in the evenings after work we hunt them in the cracks in the walls. Eventually they too begin to go extinct ...

This is how Angkar wants to see us all die: one after the other, of exhaustion, hunger and sickness — there's already almost no aspirin or quinine left. It is a gentle death sentence which costs nothing. We were informed right at the start of our captivity: "You are prisoners of war, and Angkar lacks the means to put a bullet in your head, Angkar will let you die, little by little, naturally ... "

In January, when the harvest is over, the *yautheas* distribute the paddy. They leave the villagers only the bare minimum to last until the next harvest; the rest of the stock leaves with them.

We don't hang around. In February, we have to dig ponds to catch rainwater, which is a rare and precious resource in this district. We'll learn later that these so-called reservoirs are nothing but our own graves. There is no machinery to help us so we dig and hack at the baked earth.

In March 1976, rumours are rife once more; Angkar is going to arrange to send everyone back to Phnom Penh. Again! I don't believe it anymore, because during our 'moral rearmament or education meetings' which take place every evening,

the *yautheas* order us to stop being so obsessed about returning to our homes They tell us that there is no possibility
of return, but why should that make us sad since Angkar
promises us a better life than that which we are subjected
to – sorry, which we live right now … We will soon move
again, but not to the capital. We'll only need to take a plate
or a mess tin and a spoon (where we're going there will be
no more cooking to do), two sarongs and two shirts, black
of course, a mat and a mosquito net. You always need to
have one on you to protect you against malaria. A nightmare
proposition to look forward to!

About the middle of March, we find out that Angkar is
asking the whole population (old and new) to evacuate the
villages at the foot of Phnom Traloch. The first reason given
is the imminent water shortage. The second, the extremely
bad and unsettling military situation.

They're right about the water; it's already hot and dry and
the first rains won't come until June or July. Getting hold of
a bucket of dubious coffee-coloured water is virtually impossible! Every day after work, I am forced to walk with my
poor sickly little girl to a so-called pond three kilometres
from the village. Cows and buffaloes come to wade in it,
fully-clothed men and women wash in it under the beating
sun; the barely-dried clothes are immediately covered with
dirt from the water.

After a quick wash, Jeannie and I wearily cart two buckets
of water back to the village. I hold one in my right hand
and with my left help Jeannie carry hers. We then put some
rough grains of salt in it, leave it to settle then pour off the

slightly clearer water and boil it. After all this palaver, we get some passable but salty drinkable water! It's that or dying of thirst. This awful physical and mental suffering will be forever engraved on us. Who will escape from it? It appears that those who haven't already been executed are condemned to a slow, non-violent, but certain death, which will cost Angkar nothing ...

When the new evacuations are announced, the hope that sustained the Phnom Penh refugees that they would return to their city was extinguished as quickly as it was born. Pouk Sem informs us we're going to be re-settled in Loti-Batran, on the river Loti.

7/ Loti-Batran

Loti-Batran is a few kilometres from Traloch, on an island right in the middle of the river Loti. To get there you have to cross a bridge thirty centimetres wide, so not everyone can cross at the same time, or even on the same day. While we wait our turn, we camp in a nearby pagoda which has been cleared of its monks.

In Cambodia, there are pagodas close to every village; the majority of the country is Buddhist. But under the Khmer Rouge regime they are, along with the schools and churches, considered to be the symbols of imperialism and corruption. Many monks have been massacred, or forced to marry and work in the paddy fields like everyone else.

The Muslim minority, the *Chams*, aren't treated any better. If a Khmer Rouge finds out that someone is a Muslim, they immediately issue them with pork, while the other refugees are wracked by hunger and literally dying of envy. These tyrants have absolutely no respect for religion, or even basic humanity.

After spending the night in the pagoda, we cross the bridge that straddles the river Loti to settle down in our new village. Village ... That's a bitter deception; Loti-Batran exists only in name. In reality there is nothing, not even a straw hut.

Loti-Batran is nothing more than a forest of bamboo and all sorts of different trees. "Don't worry, Angkar will take care of you, he'll give you a better life; just work and Angkar will do the rest, etc." Ah! It is the beautiful, promised land.

At the end of the morning, the *yautheas* join us in the depths of our jungle to dish out machetes and pickaxes. We are about thirty families, mostly made up of women, old people or the sick, and children who are too unwell to work. There are only a few men among the former inhabitants who manage the works, and the soldiers who watch over us. We have to clear some ground quickly to set up camp that very evening.

At dinner time, some *neary* bring us baskets of rice mixed with cooked corn. Once we have gobbled up the ladle of rice, Li and I have only one preoccupation, to get to sleep. My daughter and her little cousin start crying again, as they haven't had enough to eat and our nomadic lifestyle is starting to seriously disturb them. We try as hard as we can to get them to sleep – 'he who sleeps eats', as they say. We attach our mosquito net to four pegs before spending our first night in this place that is yet more inhospitable, even more appalling, than anything we have known until now!

As I fall asleep, I think about my son and his cousins. Where can they be? What are they doing? How are they managing to live? How are they treated and cared for if they are sick? How are they dealing with all these challenges? And Seng? How's he going to find us here, stuck in the back of beyond? The village leaders at Ta Chen assure me that our children are being well cared for, and that, when the time comes, they'll visit us ... But I no longer believe these filthy liars.

After a few days of strenuous chopping and hacking, we manage to clear around a hundred square metres for the first straw huts. While the men cut bamboo branches for the stilts, the women and those children who can hold a pickaxe dig fifty-centimetre-deep holes. We work relentlessly from six in the morning to six in the evening, with just a pause for lunch. As for breakfast, it's a long time since we knew what that was. During the harvest, our midday meal is a bowl of rice. On the Khmer Rouge's public holidays, we also get a manioc-based soup with a thumb-sized piece of pork floating in the middle. To placate our starving stomachs, we nibble minnows or tadpoles that we scavenge from the stagnant waters of the paddy fields, with a grain salt. To be permanently hungry and to watch your little eight–year–old girl slowly dying, without being able to give her anything at all, is an unbearable torment. I ask myself what I have done to the Good Lord to deserve such punishment, and everyone else as well, because I am not alone in this hellhole.

It takes several weeks to build the straw huts, and during this time we sleep out in the open. We help to make the floors out of bamboo slats that are bound together with creepers. To cover the roofs and walls, everyone (including the children) joins in making panels out of dried palm leaves and places them on bamboo slats which are then bound together with creeper. We've never seen or done any work of this kind before. It's a hard apprenticeship … but it's instructive. The only consolation is that this convict-life has taught me a lot; how to build your own house, thresh and mill paddy for white rice, plant sweet potatoes by burying little chunks of the vegetable, get bees out of their hives to collect the treasure within, a load of concrete, vital things that a city dweller is completely unaware of ... Yes, I've learned a lot, but at what price?

Soon the fruits of our labour begin to appear; each family ends up having its own 'little villa', built on poles about fifty centimetres high. Li, Ha, Jeannie and I continue to live together in the same hut, as we are still registered as one family. Here there's water close by, which is a luxury compared to the previous village. But it's still not drinkable unless it's boiled first, because we're on a closed loop in the river and we use the water for everything; to do the laundry and to wash ourselves. Moreover, in the rainy season, everything drains into the river, including the contents of the uncovered and flooded latrines. So, to protect us from illness, I always boil the river water before drinking it, mixing it with leaves from mango trees, jackfruit trees, or citronella (when we find any, because even citronella leaves have become a rare commodity). But despite these precautions, as soon as the first rains come, the refugees, already weakened by all these hardships, will be decimated like flies by sickness, a second plague in this Gehenna, to add to the famine.

Little by little all the villagers from Ta Chen are resettled in Loti and life continues on its sad course. Gangs of *yautheas* turn up unannounced and empty our bags of what little we still have – jewellery, or vital products, like soap, toothpaste and medicine. Li and I no longer have any jewellery or valuable things. All this in the name of Angkar Leu.

Once their shameful chore is done, they get on their bikes and order us, via Ta Chen, to continue clearing the forest to plant vegetables if we want to eat. We must start the plantations before the rainy season – and the floods – begin. So, according to the time of year, we'll cultivate corn, sweet potatoes, manioc, tobacco, courgettes or aubergines, all these are supposed to be our future supplies ... And yet we'll never taste another spoonful of palm sugar again, in a country that's abundant with sugar palms and in a country that used to export millions of tons of rice a year. A bowl of good whole rice will rapidly be replaced by a bowl of rice soup! – What a tragic paradox! The supplies dwindle day by day; we never catch sight of mangoes, bananas, oranges, sapodillas, papayas, etc. Where have all these good things gone?

I get weaker by the day, but I try not to let this get me down and carry on, as I must, with the clearing work. The wood is collected for the communal kitchen and, afterwards, the burnt foliage is used as a fertiliser. This work is extremely hard, especially when your body is completely worn out. I catch all the grey grasshoppers I can along my way; I have them for breakfast, lightly grilled, and they let me start without feeling empty. One morning, I'm cooking my grasshoppers in the embers under the intrigued and attentive gaze of Ta Chen's son, a lad of about eight–years–old, who's rather plump – at least compared to our poor children. He watches me, nibbling nonchalantly, without any appetite, at a large piece of grilled manioc; just the sight of it makes my mouth water. My stomach completely empty, I've just started on my insects, when the boy asks: "Is what you're eating tasty?" I shoot back: "Delicious." Then, he suggests we swap his manioc for my three measly grasshoppers ... What a good deal! Business over, I stow the precious piece of manioc away in my pocket, happy at the thought that Jeannie and Ha will have a little treat to add to the evening's ladle of rice soup.

On 15 April, it's the first anniversary of our exodus; it has already been a year, only a year, since we left Phnom Penh, a year which seems to me like a century of nightmares. The dates of the Khmer New Year (13, 14 and 15 April) are transferred to 15, 16 and 17 April, to commemorate the famous 'liberation of Kampuchea'. For this occasion, the village chief orders a pig to be slaughtered, which will be distributed to everyone: 200 grams per person in principle, but the 'old' inhabitants, it goes without saying, get a double ration.

Nevertheless, we will get three days holiday. For the first time in a year, my daughter has almost enough to eat!

And then, what a happy surprise – The Khmer Rouge allow our children, from whom we have been separated for such a long time, to pay us a visit. What a horrible shock! All of them – Jean-Jacques, Leng, Hoa and Phan – have become skeletal and weather-beaten. But without complaining, they say nothing about what they've been through. Jean-Jacques, a little lad of eleven, only tells me that he's doing man's work; he ploughs, sows, plants, harvests, digs canals, builds dykes ...

Like all the children, ours have been indoctrinated and talk only about what Angkar Pakdewat wishes. All the education we've implanted in them is wiped out; no politeness, no respect, no more "Bonjour Monsieur" or "Bonjour Madame", no "Merci".[1] They mustn't obey their parents any

---

1. As for the children of the Khmer Rouge – even the very young aged between seven and ten treat adults with insolence and contempt. Their look is often bloodthirsty and full of hate... They frighten us.

Maurice, Denise Affonço's father, sporting his medals. He had been invited by King Norodom Sihanouk to celebrate the annual Water Festival at the Royal Palace. Phnom Penh, 1953. (Affonço family album)

Maurice Affonço sets off for France. He was lent a private plane by King Norodom Sihanouk to take him on the first leg of his journey to Vietnam, from where he continued to Marseilles by boat. Phnom Penh, July 1954. (Affonço family album)

Phou Teang Seng, Denise Affonço's husband, who was taken away by the Khmer Rouge in July 1975. He was never seen again. (Affonço family album)

Khmer Rouge soldiers enter Phnom Penh, April 1975 (above and below).
(Documentation Center of Cambodia)

Jeannie, Denise Affonço's daughter,
who died of starvation on
9 November 1976, aged nine.

Hoa, Denise Affonço's niece,
who died an hour after Jeannie,
aged seventeen.

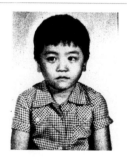

Ha, Hoa's younger brother,
who was executed at the age of
eight for stealing food.

Leng, Ha's elder sister, who died of
hunger and exhaustion in 1976 at the
age of nineteen.

THE DEAD

There is no remaining picture of Denise Affonço's sister-in-law Li, who died from cardiac oedema in 1976.

There is no remaining photograph of Li's third daughter Phan, who died of hunger in January 1977, aged thirteen.

These photographs were confiscated by Khmer Rouge soldiers, who ripped them from the author's photograph album and threw them on the ground. The photographs opposite were rescued by Denise Affonco's nieces, who hid them in their pockets.

Denise Affonço with Mme Touch Kim Seng, a student nurse, at the hospital in Siem Reap, July 1979. Denise worked here first as an auxiliary nurse and then as a washerwoman. In the distance is the well from which she drew water. (Affonço family album)

Denise Affonço with her son Jean-Jacques, then aged fifteen. This was taken during an interview with American, Cuban and Japanese lawyers before the trial of Pol Pot in absentia, organised by the pro-Vietnamese Cambodian government. They are dressed in clothes provided by the Vietnamese authorities and appear in good health thanks to the diet of multivitamins they had been fed. Phnom Penh, August 1979. (Affonço family album)

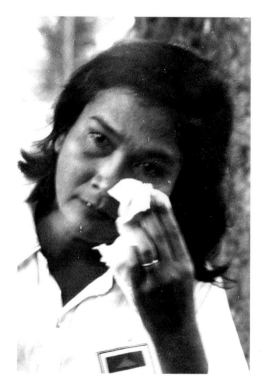

Denise Affonço during the trial of Pol Pot. Phnom Penh, 15 August 1979.
(Affonço family album)

more, but only Angkar; they're no longer our children, but theirs.

Thus, I no longer have any authority over my son, who makes it quite clear that he has no need of me and I none of him. It isn't me who feeds him, but Angkar, and not he who nourishes me, but Angkar. Sometimes, however, Jean-Jacques disobeys this rule and escapes from his camp to bring me a little bit of rice or paddy. But this isn't the way he usually behaves. The first time we see our older children again, we realise that they live in another world. All the emotional and material bonds which linked them to us are severed and destroyed. Love and affection are feelings that no longer exist in the camps, and it's the same with my daughter who stayed with me. Son, daughter, daddy, mummy, these are now meaningless terms. All values are reduced to nothing.

During the three day festivities, we are treated to two daily meetings, one at six in the morning and the other at six in the evening. In the morning, we all salute the flag of liberated Kampuchea and sing the Khmer Rouge national anthem, which I've managed to learn by writing the refrain phonetically:

Cheam krahom chea
Sroy srop tuk veal Kampuchea meatophum
Cheam Kamakors, Kaksekors dor oudom
Cheam Yutechun Yutneary Pakdevat...

Scarlet red blood
Floods the soil of the mother country Kampuchea
Precious blood of the workers, the peasants
Blood of the fighters of the revolution ...

In the evening, after dinner, the oft-speech reminds us – in case we've forgotten – that it's thanks to Angkar that we've been freed from the yoke of Lon Nol and the imperialists, thanks to Angkar that we are here to learn what we would never have learnt before. In return, we must obey Angkar's commandments and follow his code of conduct, otherwise we'll be punished ...

Does any of this blah-blah really matter? What matters to us during this brief period is the normal rice ration, the pork, a real gift from heaven, even if it's sparingly handed, the soup spoon of liquid palm sugar per person, and the spoon-ful of *prahok* – rotten fish – soaked in stinking salt, but once cooked with a chopped stalk of citronella and mixed with rice, this poor man's food becomes an immeasurable delight. After the three days of feasting, we regain some strength, and even a slight hint of optimism.

Unfortunately, our joy is short-lived. Once the feast is over, the children go back to their prison and we have to tighten our belts even more. From the end of April 1976, the bowl of proper rice becomes a ladle of rice soup once again. As for the little reserve of pork that we carefully set aside, it's gone within a few days.

It's from this point onwards, totally understandably, that members of the same family start to argue over their meagre allowance. If one gives a little more to one than the other, it immediately turns into a drama. I even argue about food on a daily basis with my easy-going sister-in-law. We're so preoccupied by our own condition that neither of us thinks about the other, or even about our children from whom we've been separated. We think only about ourselves and of Jeannie and Ha. Friendship and solidarity no longer exists even among relatives when the stomach cries out from famine.

I realise, while I am writing this, that my story is dominated by our diet; rice, lack of rice, corn, manioc, fish, salt, grasshoppers, cockroaches, scorpions, soup, *prahok*, palm sugar ... The explanation is simple. Food, and fantasizing about food, is the refugee's overriding concern, their dominant preoccupation at all times. For four years, "Are we going to eat today? What are we going to eat today?" ... There is nothing else to think about except work (which we are forced to do) and food (which is short). Nothing else. Entertainment? Well, there are the indoctrination meetings ...

This obsession eats away at us and as a result our spirits lose themselves in the past ... One day, while weeding in a manioc field, I murmur a litany of the dishes and drinks I dream about to a fellow-slave who speaks French. We are reminiscing about the famous aperitif, Dubonnet, when a *yauthea* passes by. Understanding the sense of our conversation, he warns us menacingly that if ever this 'wandering of the spirit' manifests itself again, we will be ripe for the re-education camps. Phew! That was a close shave; wasn't that officer friend of my husband's taken away simply because he insisted on speaking French?

To add to our misery and hunger, there are other problems, notably hygiene. A year after our evacuation we have no basic toiletries: no soap, no shampoo, no toothbrushes, no toothpaste. In the evening, when we get back from the paddy fields, instead of a shower, we soak ourselves fully clothed in the river, and rinse our muddy clothes at the same time. All we have left in our wardrobe are two *sampots²* and two shirts, dyed black, not even any trousers. We clean our teeth by brushing them with a bit of salt when there is any, or with sand …

This is how we have to continue to live … to survive … for three more long years. And this is without having the right to feel sorry for ourselves, to be nostalgic about the past, to laugh or even to cry over our dead. All our emotions must be suppressed deep inside ourselves. We have become robots, the living dead.

The feast is already a thing of the past. We get on with the hard task of clearing the forest. Now I'm only a shadow of my former self; I've lost so much weight that when I lie down at night on the hut floor it hurts all over, as my bones stick into my skin.

But every day I slave away so as not to lose my ration which I share with my daughter, who is as skeletal as I am. And I carry on hunting insects; I carefully bring back grasshoppers and scorpions to add to our dinner. One day, I even find a chick! The village chief's wife let her chicken out with its chicks, which wandered away close to where we were working. I managed to catch one, wring its neck and surreptitiously hide it in my pocket. Only the poor chicken saw me do it … she rushed at me, cackling with all her might, and I had to get away from the hen coops fast in order not to attract the attention of the *schlops*. That evening, when I heat up the mess tin of soup that has been distributed to us, I pop the chick in

2. The everyday skirt worn by Cambodian women.

along with some spinach leaves I've picked in a hurry on my way back. It's a veritable banquet!

Since I've been living in France, I have often thought that it really was too bad that the Parisian pigeons didn't migrate to Cambodia between 1975 and 1979, as they could have been our *plat de résistance* …

As for 'vegetables', we eat only wild spinach and water-plants picked in the wilderness. When we can't find them, we rely on the water plants that grow in the ponds which Cambodians feed to the animals, or on the roots of banana trees cut down by the former inhabitants to feed their pigs.[3]

One day, two neighbours with whom I work find a plentiful supply of bindweed, but refuse to reveal the location of this enchanted place: "Oh no, definitely not, we won't tell you, because you'll tell everyone about it and soon there'll be none left … " Alas, this is entirely my fault; when I find a little source of fish, frogs, water plants, any possibility of food, I can't keep it secret; it's better if everyone benefits from it! But famine pushes humans towards selfishness, pettiness, jealousy and squabbles, not towards sharing … In these conditions it's difficult to make any real friends. The refugees avoid getting to know each other and many of them, those who are cleverer than us, hide their real identity and professions for fear of being eliminated. In these camps, friendship has no more value than family ties.

Naturally, a diet of water plants and the like completely upsets our stomachs and leads to endless diarrhoea. After the celebrations, I'm the first to fall ill, with a form of acute dysentery (stools with blood and phlegm in them, colic and high fever), and I have no medicine to help me. Some old women advise

---

3. A piece of banana tree root is a luxury item which everyone quarrels over.

me to drink a concoction made from the bark of guava and tamarind trees, but on the first day of the crisis, I'm so feverish that I can't get myself up to go to work. I doze, shivering, under my blanket. Old Ta Chen's son, who is now a yauthea, does his rounds and spots me; he climbs into my hut without taking his sandals off and shouts down at me: "You! *Yé barang*, don't pretend to be sick, go to work otherwise you won't get anything to eat today!" Exhausted by my fever, it takes me a moment or two to get up, so the *yauthea* hauls me up by my shirt collar, and makes me get up onto my legs by kicking my backside. For better or for worse, I manage to drag myself to the cornfield, where I carry out my chores (that day, we must weed between the rows of corn) by shuffling along on my bottom as I can't stand up. Everyone can see that I'm ill, but nobody dares to say anything, so they see nothing. Everyone for himself and Angkar for all. The other women continue with the drudgery and the *neary* look jeeringly at me, without a word or any gesture of comfort. Worse, they joke among themselves and pretend that we, the corrupt of the old regime, are feigning sickness because we don't like to work the land.

There is no way to deal with the dysentery other than to drink these tisanes. Miraculously, after a week I feel a bit better, but I am completely drained, washed out, emptied.

Then, a few weeks later, I come down with malaria. The first bout is very violent and brings fever, headache, shivering fits – again there's no cure. Only the 'old' villagers, whose children are *yautheas*, have any quinine, which they swap at a high price. One quinine capsule is worth twenty boxes of rice, which obviously I haven't got tucked away.[4]

---

4. Another example: one pill of Aureomycine can be bartered for one carat of gold (36g).

I force down a concoction made out of an extremely bitter plant, the leaves of which are eaten in a salad with smoked, cured and grilled fish. After about a week, the fits become more sporadic and the illness quietens down but doesn't go away.

Today, I still ask myself where I found the physical and mental strength to put up with all these ordeals and these different illnesses, which alas, were not the last ... maybe this strength comes from my childhood? ... My mother told me that, when I was very small, we kept a goat in the garden and that I used to romp around on all fours with it. One day, when she left me alone for a few minutes, she came back to find my mouth stuffed full of goat turds, which I ate with relish. Maybe this animal matter immunised me against adversity, like some magic potion!

When the rains ccome, at the end of May or beginning of June, the ploughing starts. Every day we have to get up at three in the morning, cross the river and walk for several hours. I can't say how far Loti is from the paddy fields where they make us toil, but they border a main road – a type of *route nationale* – on which not a single car drives anymore but where we sometimes see groups of *yautheas* on foot or on bicycles, going to a neighbouring village. What I do remember is that by the time we get there the sun would just be coming up.

There are no ploughs, no oxen to carry out this task. Armed with picks, we are the oxen *and* the plough. The first hours of the morning are just about bearable; once the sun starts beating down, the work becomes more and more taxing. It is very hot and humid. Worn out by sickness and hardship, I can barely lift my pick, but – look out! – I mustn't complain about a thing. The *yautheas* watch over us, calmly seated on the side of the road, chatting and smoking their little cigarettes.

Men are a rarity in Loti-Batran. The women and children of all the men who were arrested at Koh Tukveal were deported here, and brought together with families from other camps and designated the 'families of traitors'. Those men who were left behind are taken away to the re-education camps one after the other. We all know now what assignment to these infamous camps really means – 'death by summary execution'.

I remember a Cambodian woman married to a Chinese man. She and her husband carefully hid their identities. They said that they were both native to the country and that they were fishmongers in Phnom Penh market. In reality, he was a wealthy Chinese businessman and hadn't been able to leave in time. They managed to slip through the net, until someone close to them denounced them. One evening, as was their way, the *schlops* came to get the man. That particular night several refugee families watched as their fathers or husbands left, never to return.

The next day, a *yauthea* strolled around with the scarf the Chinese man had been wearing when he was arrested wrapped round his neck. Thanks to this oh–so–subtle hint, the young wife immediately understood that she was a widow. Nonetheless, it was forbidden to cry, all the more so since her companion was a traitor – as a rich man, he was part of the corrupt, capitalist system of the old regime.

At this point, the authorities still hadn't condescended to tell me what fate had been reserved for my own traitor ...

8/ The Deaths

In August 1976, it is my sister-in-law Li's turn to fall ill. Her complexion yellows and she starts to swell up. But despite her condition, she too forces herself to go to work every day so she doesn't lose her rice ration, which she shares with Ha, her 'useless mouth'.

She gets worse. We have nothing to make her better. The lemon or jackfruit leaf concoctions which worked on me when I had nutritional oedema do nothing at all for Li, who has cardiac oedema.[1] One day, some *yauthea* pseudo-doctors come to the village to share with us their precious knowledge. In the guise of medicine, they hand out little balls of raw rice rolled in palm sugar to the sick, pretending that these will help to reabsorb the swelling – I call them 'the balls of death'. Li accepts this dubious treatment almost as if she knows what she's doing, because she's hungry and any kind of food seems like a gift from heaven. I myself beg her to give me some balls to soothe my stomach. But like everyone, she has become obsessed with food and keeps her 'precious' pills to herself. These then provoke an acute diarrhoea which is impossible to stop and will be the cause of her death.

Two days before she leaves us, I see her tenderly share

---

1. Oedema is a swelling caused by excess fluid retention.

her rice and fish with Jeannie. Li fades away gently in the evening, just before sunset, in mid-October 1976.

We must bury our dead ourselves, in the forest about a kilometre away. At nightfall, nobody wants to help me. So I have to spend the night next to the corpse, with Jeannie and Ha under the same mosquito net.

The next day I ask the neighbours for help as, weak and all alone, I'm incapable of carrying a thirty or forty kilo corpse. On top of this, there is neither wood, nor nails, nor a hammer to make a coffin. In the beginning, for the first deaths, we used bamboo slats tied together with creeper to make a sort of mat, but bamboo has now become very scarce.[2]

We put the body in an old jute sack tied up at the neck and feet, carry it to the 'cemetery', dig a hole barely a metre deep in the forest and bury Li. That is the sad end that awaits us all after our passing – and it seems increasingly close for myself and the others.

There are three or four deaths a day. Deaths from hunger, deaths from sickness and deaths from poor hygiene – the latrines that are dug close by swarm with maggots. During the rainy season, the river overflows and floods the whole village and we end up wading around in our own excrement. We live on a mudflat and drink the water which has to do for everything, including washing the clothes soiled with diarrhoea ...

---

2. Bamboo is a very precious plant. We build huts with its canes and its shoots are edible, but to cook them you have to go through a lot, as they are hidden away in the middle of clumps of the plants and you often come out covered in grazes. This is what happened to Jean-Jacques; one day he came back to the village with two beautiful shoots in his *kromar* (scarf), but his shirt completely in tatters and his back covered in scratches. The Khmer Rouge ended up forbidding the cooking of bamboo shoots because, being denuded like this, the plants stopped growing.

Forced to rub shoulders with death and lacking the barest
essentials, we end up committing food crimes, without even
thinking that we are risking capital punishment. One day,
while picking wild spinach and water plants, I come across a
little vegetable plot overflowing with aubergines.[3] Thinking
the place is deserted, I sneak in, crawling beneath the little
trees and promptly begin to pick some and stuff my pockets
– the pockets of our black blouses are very useful. The moment that I re-emerge from the field on all fours I find myself
nose to nose with a *schlop*. The offence is obvious. Sniggering
spitefully, he immediately takes me to see to the village chief.
As the latter is absent, he hands me a pickaxe and orders me:
"There, *yé barang*, you can weed this plot while you wait for
the chief to come back." Scared to death, I say nothing and
set to work. After about an hour, the *schlop* comes back with
a fellow sidekick. With no explanation whatsoever, the two
guards order me to get into a little boat and take me across
the river to a nearby village where I have to appear before
the head chief, a leader I've never seen before in Loti. The
crossing doesn't take more than a few minutes but it is made
in an oppressive silence, that is broken only by the sloshing
of the water against the oars. Sitting between the two, not
knowing what they intend to do, I shiver with fear. I blame
myself for having been so foolish and bitterly regret that I
stupidly let myself get caught.

The head chief, who I set eyes on for the first time, starts
by staring at me maliciously, then asks abruptly:

---

3. We plant and take care of all the vegetables, but once they are ripe and harvested
we never see them again – with the exception of the corn, manioc and sweet potatoes that are redistributed to us. Courgettes, pumpkins, tomatoes and aubergines
vanish into thin air ... or rather into the cooking pots of the wives of the Khmer
Rouge chiefs.

"Why do you steal?"

Pathetically, I reply:

"Because I'm hungry!"

Dryly, he retorts:

"But we're hungry too, and yet we don't steal ... "

While he lectures me, a lovely smell of grilled fish wafts from his hut, tickling my nostrils agreeably and torturing my poor empty stomach a bit more. Then I see, through the half-opened door, his wife and children sitting in a circle around a big bowl of steaming soup, eating noisily, helping themselves to laden handfuls of rice and pieces of grilled fish. I drool, I seethe with anger, but cannot break my silence. And the sermon continues: "You, the intellectuals, you're really hopeless; we can't look after such rotten elements!" At these words, I realise what's in store for me, and forgetting all their taboos, I start to cry real tears: I ask the chief to pardon me, I promise that I'll never do it again, that I'll try to re-educate myself ... Nothing seems to move this big shot! Unperturbed, he turns to the *yautheas* who brought me: "Take her away!" and indicates the direction from which no one ever returns ...

At this very moment Ta Yem, the *canaksrok*, head of the district, turns up on a bicycle. When he's told what's going on, he asks me about my family and origins and then he asks if I should like to return to France. I reply: "*Mith*, my fate lies with Angkar's decision ... " It seems to me that is what one must say; in some way I know how to bend with the wind.

There are a few minutes of heavy silence. I tremble like a dead leaf; I think how stupid I am to have got myself in such a fix just for the sake of a few aubergines. But when you're driven by hunger ... The verdict comes at last: "This time, you are pardoned, but if there's a next time, Angkar will take appropriate measures."

Phew! That day, I escaped death and I thank God I'm still alive. But that very evening, at the 'brain-washing' meeting, I must criticize myself in front of everybody. I explain what I did, I implore Angkar and my comrades to pardon me, I promise never to steal again and I ask that Angkar should eliminate me if I err once more ... I bend, I don't break, but what humiliation!

Not everyone is as lucky as me at this little game. One day, my son and some other children are given forty-eight hours leave from their camp and they come to see us in Loti. The chief's wife, who's in charge of the communal kitchen, takes advantage of their presence to get some extra help, and she sends three boys, of which one is Jean-Jacques, to gather firewood for cooking. They must cut branches or tree trunks. The children leave, each furnished with a machete. Despite everything, children will be children. On the way, they come across a pile of wood that has already been cut. So to speed things up and in order not to have to work too hard, they help themselves from the pile ... but when they are doing this, two *yautheas* take them by surprise and deal with them as if they are thieves. They're immediately arrested and taken to the far end of the island where there is a manioc plantation.

When I get back from the fields in late afternoon, I notice the boys haven't come back from collecting wood. Not knowing what's happened, I go to look for them with another mother. When we get close to the plantation, we see our children digging away, crying silently. We daren't do anything, we wait. Just before sunset the boys are freed. I welcome back my son with immense relief … but also with bemusement, anger, and a painful inability to do anything. Jean-Jacques and his companions have been lectured to like thieves, called the children of traitors and the irredeemably corrupt, they have been beaten with manioc canes, then forced to work from ten in the morning until evening, with nothing to eat or drink. Jean-Jacques' body is covered with marks from the blows … But my child doesn't complain, doesn't cry, doesn't say a word. He closes himself up completely.

I still feel terrible when I think of what happened to my son, a twelve–year–old boy whom these ordeals forced to grow up too fast; to become adult without having the time to experience the innocence of childhood. The treatment he endured that day – and certainly at other times which I didn't witness, and he never wanted to talk to me about – all these abuses have scarred him so much that on returning to a normal life, for years, he could not bear to see scenes of beatings at the cinema or on television. If he ever randomly came across a scene of that kind, he would instantly change the channel, and at night he had nightmares and cried in his sleep.

"Don't steal! Don't be corrupt!" The dictators in charge want us to adopt their codes of conduct as they have been adopted by the local population who has been converted to their cause, so we will also become a pure and hard people … The 'older' villagers chosen to instil these rules in us are often cruel, but also far from irreproachable, as they show they are incapable of following their own commandments!

We know perfectly well that they lie when they pretend that they eat like us; in fact, they embezzle the rice supplies to eat themselves. Their scheming is sometimes discovered. Van, the son-in-law of the village chief, soon after he replaced his father as team leader, will be dismissed for stealing rice. But he won't be punished nor will he have to criticize himself in public.

The wife of this same chief can help herself to our supplies with impunity and no-one reproaches her. She's pregnant and, grabbed by sudden cravings, she regularly pays a visit to the vegetable patches – which we have planted with such difficulty, cared for and watered before and after our hard days of collective labour – to swipe our courgettes and ripe ears of corn.

I've managed to make 'my own' vegetable patch; by forcibly repeating to myself that if I don't want to die of hunger, I only had to plant one myself, I've laid out a little patch in front of my hut where I've sowed about ten maize plants, a bed of sweet potatoes and a few courgettes. But plants don't sprout by themselves – they must be watered every morning and every evening. So before I go to the fields I get up half an hour early, around three o'clock in the morning, to draw water from the river. My strength diminishes day by day, it's exhausting work when one is already doing forced labour, but I drive myself to do it, persuading myself that this way I can eat when I'm hungry. Just the idea that my efforts will be rewarded gives me the strength to carry out this extra task. And, indeed, after a few weeks, my corn has cobs and my courgettes flowers. One morning, I happily contemplate my beautiful vegetable patch with satisfaction and I rejoice: "Great! They're ripe – this evening we can add to our soup ration!" When I am on my way out, I warn Jeannie and Ha to keep a close eye on the treasure to make sure no one tries to steal them. But, when I get back at the end of the day, what a terrible disappointment awaits me! There are no more courgettes, no more corn and all the leaves of the sweet potato plants are ripped off. The children could do nothing; the guilty party is the wife of the village chief! On the pretext that Madame is pregnant, she has paid a visit to all the vegetable patches and taken everything she fancied. She told the children that her loot would go into the communal soup for dinner. In the evening, of course, when we are issued our ladle of white rice soup there's nothing else in it, not a single trace of the vegetables, the precious fruits of our hard labour. They have lied to us again ... But where are these famous pure and hard people? I'm in physical and mental despair, and totally exhausted, but I can't complain to my torturers. I'm at their mercy.

My sister-in-law has gone to a far better world than the one in which we survive with such difficulty. Where she is, she doesn't suffer anymore, whereas for me and the rest of the family the Calvary continues. I am now responsible not only for my nephew, but also for my nieces, Leng, Hoa and Phan, who soon return to the village, sick and weak, and I must tell them about their mother's death ... They hardly react to the sad news. It's as if after all the daily brainwashing where they hear that they are the children of Angkar and have no further need of their parents, they are no longer touched by loss. Leaving that aside, the three girls are in a very bad way. Ill and worn out, they are in no state to work, and because of their lack of productivity are therefore only entitled to half-rations. As for my own girl, who every day becomes more skeletal and more fragile, she has always been considered a 'useless mouth' by the authorities.

Jean-Jacques, who is also much thinner and has stopped growing, holds on, or at least so it seems ... He remains at a camp for children of his age, Kasang-ôt-Krop, a few kilometres from Loti, where he is finishing the harvest, treated as if he were an adult and doing the same work for the same meagre rice ration. I know he doesn't have the time to be really miserable as he thinks only of working to survive.

As for me, it's my turn to swell up all over – I'll find out later from the Vietnamese doctors that, in contrast to my sister-in-law who suffered from a cardiac oedema, which is impossible to cure without the appropriate medicine, I have a renal condition, which is less serious. Despite my state, I continue to go to the fields to earn my daily rice ration, which I share with the two youngsters.

The 'old' villagers give us advice on how to cure the swellings, but from a distance; if somebody suffering from oedema climbs up to their hut, they chase them away with swipe of a broomstick.[4] These ignorant people think the illness is infectious. They recommend that we drink all sorts of magic potions made up of seven young bamboo leaves picked with the morning dew, seven dried jackfruit leaves and seven lemon grass leaves.[5] This tisane does nothing for Leng, Hoa, Phan, or Jeannie. On the other hand it has some beneficial effects on me, as a diuretic, but does not cure me completely.

---

4. As for the so-called *yauthea* doctors, they sometimes pass by to distribute handfuls of magic pills, but they never go into the houses where they know there are sick people.
5. Seven is a lucky number. The jackfruit, a highly perfumed fruit, should be eaten when it is very ripe. The stones are edible once they've been boiled. Normally, you could find them everywhere but under the Khmer Rouge we never saw them.

My bouts of malaria continue, during which I have no right to favourable treatment. On the contrary, the 'old' villagers drive us on with no consideration. They are hard and cruel, just like Van, Ta Chien's son-in-law who, before he was caught red-handed and stripped of his powers, was both *schlop* and team leader. As remorseless with men as with women, he would repeat incessantly: "Angkar wishes you to learn to work in all weathers, in sun, rain, wind, storms, nothing must stop you, not even sickness; you must harden yourselves." Under his orders, we all get on with it, come rain or shine. During bouts of malaria, I must continue planting the paddy fields, all the while shivering with fever under a blazing sun, sometimes in torrential rain and always standing in water halfway up my calves.[6] All the protection I have against bad weather is an old yellow oilskin mackintosh I've managed to hide from the constant confiscations, which does the job well enough.

One morning, I'm flattened by a particularly severe fit. Stretched out on the floor of the hut, incapable of getting up, I shiver feverishly under my old blanket and two old jute sacks (even if I had had ten around my shoulders, I would still have been cold); to make me feel better, I need something extremely heavy on top of my body. So I ask my daughter – who's so light! – sitting sadly by my side, to climb onto my back. Poor Jeannie, herself weak and tortured by hunger, refuses. In a fit of anger, I stretch my leg out and give her a violent kick which makes her fall under the hut. How could I have behaved like this towards my own child? When I think about it today, that scene cuts me to pieces ...

---

6. There is a type of paddy that you can transplant in flooded paddy fields. We had two harvests a year.

It isn't only sickness that we have to watch out for, but accidents at work ... In our lives as corrupt town dwellers, we have never learned the proper way to use a sickle for the harvest, or a pickaxe; these rustic chores often end up as an assault course.

One day, while I'm turning the baked earth in a manioc field, I cut the ligament in my big toe. I don't have any antiseptic and nothing to stop the bleeding. The 'old' villagers advise me to urinate on the wound and then apply a poultice made out of the seeds of a wild herb which grows all over the place. The effect is miraculous. But since we always walk bare foot and I continue to wade in the mud, the wound doesn't get better and becomes infected a few days later. My foot starts to swell up and I have a fever. I fear tetanus. I continue applying the poultice for several weeks. I can hardly walk, but I have to *to sou*, not stop work, I must carry on going back to the stagnant water in the paddy fields. At the end of the month, I don't know how, but the wound heals, as if by miracle ...

My life as a savage has taught me that urine is not only a very useful disinfectant but also a manure. To make an effective fertiliser for the vegetable patch or tobacco plants, you must leave the liquid in a jar for forty-eight hours and then dilute it with an equal quantity of water. Thanks to this technique, we get magnificent crops of tobacco, courgettes and corn ...

On 9 November 1976 Jeannie and Hoa die, within an hour of each other.

The weeks that lead up to the loss of my daughter are very difficult. More and more torn apart by hunger, she becomes irritable, bad-tempered and naughty. Every day, she goes to beg from the village chief's wife, waiting to see if she will give her any leftovers, or dashing to pick up anything she throws out for her dog. When she gets hold of a bit of manioc or a handful of grilled rice, she scurries away to eat it secretly without letting her cousins – who are themselves hungry and who might well fight her for it – see what she is doing. On one of the days that manioc is handed out, I make the mistake of giving Jeannie a slightly tinier piece than my nephew; she thinks it's unfair and is infuriated. She calls me all sorts of names ... Hunger can make anyone lose their mind. But can one act differently when one is actually dying from it?

My daughter isn't the only one obsessed by food. Take the time, after the manioc harvest, when I went back to the harvested field with Jeannie and Ha and, between the three of us, we managed to scavenge about a kilo of broken manioc roots, still buried in the ground. When we get back, we have a little feast and everyone agrees to save a few pieces for the next day, which I hide carefully under my pillow.[7] While I was asleep, Hoa, who was also tortured by hunger, stole them and ate them raw.

The following day we woke up, cheerfully for once, knowing that we had something to put in our mouths. But we were brutally disappointed; the bag is found, empty, under the hut. Furious, we all accused each other until Hoa confessed to her wrongdoing ...

On the morning of the day of her death, Jeannie wakes me

---

7. At the time I hid everything, even big grains of salt which had become gold nuggets.

around three o'clock to ask if she can have a little rice later on. The evening before, Angkar had actually promised to increase our ration. I tell her that I'll have some rice; I'll give it to her myself. Then she says she is sorry for misbehaving over the size of her piece of manioc root: "Tell me, Maman, can you forgive me for yesterday evening? I know I wasn't nice to you." I reply, heartbroken and with tears in my eyes, that it's already forgotten and that she mustn't worry about it. Inside, I know that it won't be much longer, as they say that before dying, people change; either they become very gentle and ask forgiveness from those around them or very mean so that they regret nothing. On the verge of despair, I don't know how to grant her wish. At this precise moment, I don't need a doctor or medicines, only a bowl of rice for a little nine-year-old girl who's dying of starvation, nothing but a bowl of rice. To helplessly watch your child slowly die of starvation is an unbearable torture …

That day, we are excused from work in the fields. To pass the time, as I have no other way of helping her until we get our rice ration, I give her a little wash to start the day and change her. Then I rush to gather some dead wood to prepare her a tisane of lemongrass leaves.

Not long after I leave, little Ha runs to find me. Jeannie is in a very bad way. I hurry back. She is already breathing with difficulty. With a heavy heart, I realise that there is nothing more that I can do. She can no longer hear me. Helpless, my heart broken by the pain, I help her in her slow agony by taking her hand, as if to guide her along the path to a better world. She fades away softly in the middle of the morning.

For a long time I sit there, immobile, neither daring to cry or to say a prayer to put her soul to rest. Overwhelmed by sorrow, I'm paralyzed and continue to stare at her skeletal, lifeless, little body.

Hoa's rasping breath calls me back to reality. She too is dying ... That morning I had also washed and changed her. For a week now she has been in bed, debilitated by the diarrhoea brought on by those balls of rice which no tisane can stem. To cure her swellings, the criminal doctors of the Khmer Rouge gave her these cursed balls of palm sugar-coated rice bran which for two days give you the impression of being full up but then trigger terrible diarrhoea, which, if it's not stopped in time, can lead to death from dehydration. The Khmer Rouge potion cures one sickness but only induces another far more terrible. The infernal circle – swelling, ball of bran, diarrhoea – leads directly to paradise. These monsters know very well what effect their perverse treatments have. For them it's a cheap and efficient way of gradually eliminating us. After each death, I hear the *yautheas* and the 'old' villagers sneering: "Well there you are! They die because they only eat dirt, rice bran and wild spinach!" Dirt – that is something we would gladly do without ...

So my niece fades away an hour after my daughter, under my empty gaze. So many emotions on the same day plunge me into a trance. For hours, I can do nothing, happy to stare into the void, as if the world has stopped turning. No prayers to put their souls to rest, no ceremony. We die like animals; we are buried like animals, with no graves. To bury the two corpses, I must ask my neighbours for help, because I don't have the strength to dig two holes. I'm so numbed by death that it is as if I am made of marble. I do not shed a single tear. Anyway, it is categorically forbidden to cry, just as it is forbidden to show any happiness. But who would want to laugh or sing after two years like this? In the village there is no sound of laughter or shouts of children playing. You can still see a few of them, but they are sick children, 'useless mouths' who roam about like zombies searching for anything they can eat ...

That year, Loti Batran resembles a city of death. Death touches every family. In the evening, you can hear the moans and suffering cries of the sick. In the morning, out come one or two corpses from the huts. Most of the refugees are dying of exhaustion and sickness. The plot of earth cleared to pass as a burial ground quickly fills up; another one must be found.

None of these deaths move the Khmer Rouge in the least. One *yauthea* goes so far as to say: "So what if they snuff it, they're corrupt and rotten, the less there are, so much the better. Angkar won't have to sort out anymore problems with the rice .. ."

The famine gets more and more dire, it torments everyone. It's a slow but unbearable torture. Sweet potato leaves remain a luxurious commodity. I stuff myself with all sorts of creepers, thorny, wild spinach, bulrushes and the roots of banana trees cut down by the *yautheas* after they have gathered the fruits.[8] The bindweed doesn't even grow anymore – we devoured it all. To get the sensation that I've eaten a little meat, I fall back on grasshoppers, scorpions, centipedes and cockroaches. Some people even risk eating manioc leaves, which can contain a deadly poison. It's a lottery – sometimes you pick the leaves of a healthy plant, and sometimes you come across a contaminated one, and then, it's guaranteed

---

8. The bulrushes, once dried, are used to make mats.

vomiting, diarrhoea and death …

My swelling is always there. Physically I'm completely used up, but I work as best I can. Clearing the forest or weeding the plantations gives me a chance to look for a few grasshoppers or termites.

I even end up searching for food under the village chief's hut, or rather picking up the leftovers which he tosses to his dog, as his place is overflowing with rice and fish. In the evening, once I've gulped down my ladle of soup, I take up my vigil near his hut and wait patiently for the family to finish their meal. The moment they chuck out the leftovers through the kitchen floorboards I get under there before the pigs and the dog, and collect all that I can; pieces of manioc or sweet potato, fish heads, one or two handfuls of rice. This is how, one day, I get bitten by the dog. He gets there before me, and when I try to grab the piece of cow hide he's gnawing, he snaps at me … Hunger is a physical torture, an insidious, mental cruelty that makes you lose all thoughts of dignity, of hygiene, and brings man down to the level of an animal. I'm surprised one beautiful morning when I see my neighbour gulping down huge earthworms, having split them open with a knife, cleaned the dirt off and boiled them. I've tried everything, but earthworms I could never touch, even though my neighbour assured me that they were 'edible' …

In December 1976, harvesting begins again and brings with it the luxury of solid rice for those two or three months. This hope gives us a little good cheer.

The same month, it's the turn of nineteen–year–old Leng, my dead sister-in-law Li's eldest daughter, to die. She didn't suffer from swellings or diarrhoea. She just got steadily thinner, had no periods for two years, and weakened daily. Bizarrely, she has a premonition of the precise day it will happen and seems completely calm.

One morning, Leng announces: "Auntie, I have no strength left," and goes to bed. I look after her and wash her linen, as, no longer able to get up, she has done it in her trousers. She cries on seeing me clean her dirty things; she does not want me to, but I must, since we all only have two changes of clothes left.

Two days later, a few hours before she dies, she tells her younger brother, Ha, and her second sister, Phan, to be good and not cause me too many worries otherwise she'll come and find them after her death. She then tells me that she doesn't feel clean and asks me if I can wash her and put her in the white sampot and shirt recently handed out by Angkar, that we haven't yet had time to dye black. While I'm fulfilling her last desires, she confides: "Auntie, if I don't go tonight, I will tomorrow. Don't worry! When I'm up there, could you please just make sure that I'm properly buried? The hole must be deep and you must put me in there yourself, so that nobody steals my clothes and the wild beasts don't eat my body."

Nearly thirty years on, I still shiver when I recall her words. If my niece asked me to do this, it was because she had seen with her own eyes bodies disinterred by wild animals, and others by grasping grave robbers who dug them up, to get rice in exchange for their clothes ...

After we settle her last wishes, Leng says she is tired and would like to rest. "They'll come to find me," she adds. Then she shuts her eyes, as if to sleep, and passes away peacefully at nightfall. Having neither candle nor paraffin for a vigil, I put her under the same mosquito net as myself, where we spend the night beside her brother and sister.

Nobody is frightened of death or corpses any more.

So I scrupulously follow Leng's instructions; I dig a hole two metres deep instead of one metre and do everything myself right down to burying her body. After this macabre and exhausting task, I get on with work as if nothing has happened. There are only three of us left in the hut now; Ha, aged seven, Phan, twelve, who's also suffering from general swelling, and me.

Around this time my Chinese neighbour also loses her children, four boys, one after another. Psychologically very frail, she can't cope with such a blow and goes completely mad. Since our arrival at Loti – where we met – she's never taken part in the forced labour, on the pretext that she's too physically weak. Strangely, the Khmer Rouge leave her in peace. When we go to the fields, she stays in bed, moping over her past, and not really connecting with other people …

One day, exhausted on the way back from the fields, my stomach empty, I saw her, surrounded by her boys, noisily eating some hot, good quality rice, accompanied by grilled fish. Just the smell of it gave me stomach cramps … Jeannie looked on sadly, drooling. But at no point did my neighbour have the kindness to give her even just one ball of rice. They contented themselves with turning their backs on my poor little girl and continued to stuff their faces. Remembering this scene still breaks my heart.

This woman had lots of jewellery, so could get the daily ration without working. By exchanging her gold she got enough to eat. But how did she manage to hide all her treasures? Why did the evil *yautheas* always leave her in peace? Did she bribe them? There are lots of questions that I still ask myself today.

In spite of these arrangements, she couldn't keep up. That very year, 1976, the year of my deaths, her four sons all died, although they were better fed than most of the other children. And then she herself went in her turn.

The river level starts to drop in November, leaving some dry land behind the house, so I can start another vegetable patch. If nobody steals it, I shall have a little extra to add to the daily ladle of soup. So I have the added chore of watering it, morning and evening. I spur myself on: "Come on Denise, go on, hang in there ... " and the thought of picking the fruits of my own labour gives me superhuman resolve and physical strength. At night, when hunger pains keep me awake, I get up, suck a grain of coarse salt, drink a big bowl of fresh water and water my cottage garden by the light of the moon. The work and the prospect of fruit and vegetables preoccupies me and keeps me going. I say over again like a refrain: "Denise, don't die, stay alive to be a witness to all these atrocities; the world must know what's happening here ... You must do this for your children and for the loved ones you've lost ... "

1977 arrives. I try desperately to care for my third niece, but Phan does not get better and she too gives up her soul one January morning. On that day, as a sign of mourning for all my loved ones who have died – and also because I have so many head lice – I decide to shave my head. At first I tried putting petrol on my head, but the vile beasts have bred so fast that a radical solution is needed. So an old village woman shaves my head with a kitchen knife ...

After all these emotions, I tell myself that a little dip in the river will give me a bit of a tonic. But while trying to avoid a leech, I slip and lose my footing. Not knowing how to swim, I'm in danger of drowning. There's nobody nearby and I ransack my brain frantically and try to remember the few strokes that I learned at school ... I finally manage to get back to dry land ... and to my nightmarish life. Bizarrely, despite the slow torture that we suffer daily, we cling on to life. Death would have been a deliverance – but I don't want to die yet. The weaker I get physically the steelier my resolve becomes. For whom? Why?

9/ Reorganisation and Calamity

Since the beginning of our exodus we have been completely cut off from the world. Everything is blocked, not a single item of news from the outside world gets through to us. We don't even know what is happening inside the country, the political decisions the leaders are taking or the attitudes of other nations towards what we are living through ...

All the same, even in our narrow prison we notice, or rather feel, some changes in the way our gaolers behave and this often has dramatic consequences on our daily lives.

Towards the end of the gloomy year of 1976, the Khmer Rouge devise a big general reorganisation. All the villages are regrouped into *sahakârs* (co-operatives). Four *sahakârs* make up a *sangkat* (district) and six *sangkats* a *daumbaung* (a county).

For us, the villages of Ta Chen, Ta Svay, Ta Krak and Ta Lim are put together in a *sahakâr* and at its head a chief is appointed. He's called Ta Man, and he's a merciless *yauthea*. In turn, the *sahakârs* of Phnom Leap, Loti, Mean Doul and Prey Chou form the *sangkat* of Phnom Leap, which, with five others, is part of *daumbaung* No. 5, in the province of Battambang. From now on, if I'm asked where I live, I must reply *sahakâr* Loti, *sangkat* Phnom Leap.

Ta Chen, Ta Svay, Ta Krak and Ta Lim are all relieved of their functions as village chiefs. The stocks of rice, salt, sugar and fish are gathered under the care of the despotic Ta Man, who manages them himself with the help of a *peanich* (storekeeper).

The reorganisation doesn't improve the rice ration … at midday and in the evening we are entitled to our ladle of watery soup, out of which we can barely fish a spoonful of rice. Ta Man, however, promises us wonderful things: "Be patient, dear comrades, next year you'll have three meals a day and you'll eat good solid rice."

Despite this encouraging speech, the next year, naturally, we will be short of everything …

The other major change is that, from the beginning of January 1977, cooking for ourselves is no longer permitted. They no longer distribute sweet potatoes, manioc or dried fish, and all those who have personal rice supplies must give them to the village chief. It's absolutely forbidden to cook anything at all, with the exception of the water we drink and the soup we are permitted to make from the wild plants we gather. But cooking rice is a crime that will be severely punished; if we put some in a cooking pot, it shows we have some, and if we do, then we must have stolen it …

Angkar does our cooking! A canteen worker takes the 'midday snack' directly to the workers in the fields. For old people or children left in the village, the first meal is around ten or eleven in the morning. When the bell rings, they rush with their mess tins and spoons to a shelter called 'the dining room'. The cook (normally the village chief's wife) hands out bowls of solid rice as thankfully it's the harvest season – once the harvest is over there will only be soup on the menu. Then grown-ups and children sit on benches in groups of four at a long table, in front of a bowl of 'fish soup'. In fact, it is an opaque liquid based on *prahok* with just two or three pieces of manioc or banana root floating in it. Everyone throws themselves on it like a horde of starving dogs, and the bowls are clean in a few minutes. It's the same thing at the second meal of the day, at five o'clock.

For important occasions or feast days, like New Year, a pig is sometimes slaughtered, but in the bowl of soup to be shared by four people, there are just four pathetic little bits of unrecognisable meat. The cook and the *yautheas* keep the best pieces for themselves.

I'm always as hungry as a wolf and I would be capable of eating a kilo of rice at every meal. I try to get myself transferred to threshing the paddy; the work is much harder than harvesting, but those assigned to it get a larger ration, and can also salvage some rice bran, an extremely welcome extra.

The period of plenty during the harvest doesn't last long. Towards the end of February, the village starts to run out of supplies. At the time I didn't know what was behind this cruel disruption to our food supplies. Once out of the camps, I will learn that a part of the rice we harvested with the sweat of our brows was sent to China in exchange for arms, munitions and lorries ... We live in a rice-producing country yet we are reduced to dying of hunger at the will of the Khmer Rouge.

When there is no more rice to thresh, the women are sent into the forest to cut a plant called *tien khêt* which, once chopped up, mixed with cow dung and dried, can be used as a fertilizer. This work is overseen by Ta Sok, another maniac as cruel and heartless as his associates. Apparently he joined the Khmer Rouge long before 1975, and speaks several languages: French, English, Thai and Chinese. He obviously finds me disagreeable as, every time he sees me, he never ceases needling me during work: "So, *yé barang*, would you work like this in your country? Do you like what Angkar is doing?"… I reply with the corny old tune: "Oh yes, I find all the things that Angkar teaches us very useful, all these things I would never have learned in France …"

I'm assigned to making fertilizer for about a month. Every day, the 'production overseer', the notorious Ta Sok, tells us: "You must endeavour to make as much as possible for our rice fields; Angkar needs six tonnes for the whole *sangkat!*"

The gathering of *tien khêt* really is hard labour. The day starts at six in the morning. As soon as the bell sounds, we must all be ready in front of Pouk Sok's house with our machetes, then we head off in the direction of the forest and walk around for an hour before we find the accursed plant. We must each cut forty kilos a day, to tie in twenty kilo bales, which we bring back balanced on our heads. If a bale is less than twenty kilos – they weigh it by hand and guess – we are punished. On return, we cut up the stems into little pieces, then go to find cowpats to mix in with the chopped *tien khêt*. On each trip around twenty kilos of dung has to be carted along and, in one afternoon, we make at least five trips. Finally, we mix the plant and the cow dung together, and pour our urine – which has been collected and stored for this purpose – over it. Every morning we bring it to the place where the fertilizer is made.

Once it's mixed, we leave it to dry for a few days before taking it to the paddy fields; that's one hundred and twenty to one hundred and fifty kilos a day per person. The fields are far away and it is man's work ... Yet, when the labour force is lacking – with the repetitive purges, men are nearly extinct – children of five or six are called up! The older kids – seven to ten years old – aren't called up, because they are apparently grouped together to learn to read and write. In reality, they are used to cut the *tien khêt*, harvest and plant ...

The youngsters work under the supervision of an older boy, who is one of the 'old' villagers, and is treated as an adult.[1] Accidents are frequent. One day, going to find *tien khêt*, a child of seven dies after being bitten by a viper. Another time, finding no plants left in the usual place, the supervisor took a whole group in a canoe to the opposite village. They found plenty to pick, but on the way back the overloaded canoe capsized and sank and several children were drowned. The kids are also exploited to mind the cows and collect their dung to make fertiliser. All a long way from learning how to read ...

Under Ta Man's reign as president of the *sahakâr*, executions multiply. It spells big trouble for you if they find out that you were a soldier, held an important position in the old re-gime, or if you had a mistress or two wives. The *yautheas* will come and get you straight away and you will never be seen again. Under the old, so-called 'corrupt' regime, bigamy was allowed and even legalised. Under the Khmer Rouge it is forbidden and adultery is severely punished. On the other hand, if a Khmer Rouge wants to marry a young refugee she doesn't have the right to refuse – if she does, she is con-

---

1. The key posts such as team leader, warehouse keeper, cook or spy were always reserved for 'old' inhabitants, even if they were children.

demned to death. Many young girls from Phnom Penh are thus forced to marry wounded Khmer Rouge soldiers; they are Angkar's rewards for its valiant warriors.

In Ta Man's village there was a beautiful young woman from Phnom Penh who seemed well off. She had developed malaria on her arrival on the island, and never worked. One day, while chatting with her, I discover that she was a professor of philosophy at the Lycée Sisowath, in Phnom Penh. In fact, she feigns the malaria symptoms to avoid participating in the communal work. She also pretends to the *yautheas* that she is dumb and only talks with gestures.

In the end, her behaviour encourages the *schlops* to keep an eye on her. They raid her hut one evening when she has not attended the re-education meeting. She is caught writing in a little notebook the account of what she has witnessed since April 1975. The very next morning two torturers, barely sixteen years old, take her to the 'forest to the west' for a one way trip; no one who has ever been taken there ever returns. The young woman has her throat savagely cut. Once their filthy deed is done, the *schlops* come back to loot her hut, where they find gold, diamonds and precious stones.

At the evening education meeting, the village chief tells us that Angkar has found an enemy of the regime in the village and that she has been dealt with as she deserved. This 'philosopher' was nothing but a disruptive and corrupt element, the worst type of intellectual who had conserved the bad habits of the old regime ... after all, didn't she hoard gold and precious stones?

Then I realised how she had managed to survive for so long without working. Just like my ex-neighbour, the young woman bartered her gold for rice and fish.

Naturally the jewels go straight to Angkar's coffers, in this case, those of Ta Man.

In 1977 the disruptions go on.

Later I learn from the archives that at a national level the Khmer Rouge are divided into pro-Vietnamese and pro-Chinese camps, and the Cambodian military units faithful to the latter are making numerous raids into the Vietnamese border provinces. This situation presumably has an effect on our masters because in March, just as we are beginning the rice harvest again, the village chief announces the arrival of *nearadey*, inhabitants from the south-west. Thus, three thousand people are spread out across daumbaung No.5. Loti's *sahakâr* gets ten families; as a result our village inherits Ta Suong, who becomes our storekeeper, and Ta Soy, who becomes the new *sahakâr* president instead of Ta Man. Two families are now responsible for the village of Ta Chen: the family of Ta Ling and that of his brother-in-law.

Ignorant as usual about what's happening at the top, we are delighted, convinced the arrival of the *nearadey* will make our lives better. Alas, not long after these people have settled in, the reprisals double in intensity and our disappointment is immense.

At first, however, in order to get us to talk, the new chiefs act very paternalistically towards us. Ta Soy tours round all the villages to inspect what state they are in, visiting the sick, distributing medicine (pills that look a bit like Chinese medicines, which are said to cure everything). When he discovers that the cemetery is full, he acts as if he is shocked, and feigns ignorance that there have been so many deaths.

He asks questions like: "But what did they die from?" And everyone is eager to tell him what we have endured – the famine, the sicknesses and to complain, explaining how the 'old' villagers have treated us unjustly ... In fact, everyone thinks these new chiefs who show an interest in our plight will help us to get out of this hellhole. It's a fatal error. We fall blindly into their trap, not imagining these monsters' cruel little game.

Not long after the *nearadey* arrive, there is a big gathering of all the inhabitants of the villages in the *sahakâr*. Ta Soy announces that he has been sent by Angkar to take care of the population in place of the previous leaders, a band of traitors who did not follow Party orders. Angkar sent us rice, salt, milk, soap, medicine and even cotton fabric, and all these were embezzled ... "From now on," Ta Soy claims, "your life will be better. You will have a day of rest every ten days. This will be devoted to education meetings so that you can become better trained. On those days, we will kill an ox and you'll even be entitled to a dessert. And when you work, you'll have the right to two breaks of fifteen minutes, morning and afternoon ..."

The life these new rules promise seems idyllic. For us it's the beginning of Paradise!

As far as the rice soup is concerned (which he hasn't changed), Ta Soy announces: "Have courage, my dear comrades, you must continue to struggle a little longer, as Angkar is still in need. *Pracheachun* (you, the people), you're not getting the maximum yield from the paddy fields. To help you, Angkar has decided to build a large dyke at O'Leap which will carry to all the fields. When we are masters of our work, masters of the water and masters of the earth, you'll then be able to have your three meals a day, have enough to eat, and you'll only work two hours a day."

So be it. That day, everyone wants to believe such beautiful words. I myself start to dream again of a better future. At the end of the meeting, his team ask each of us to fill in a curriculum vitae (again!), apparently so that Angkar can know which work to entrust us with.

I don't hide the fact that I'm French and that I've worked at the French Embassy, as I still have this foolish hope that France is searching for its citizens. Life in Phnom Penh must surely have got back to normal by now?

In full confidence, we note down scrupulously our old ways of life, and it all disappears into oblivion. A few months later, those few men who have survived previous purges all disappear in their turn. Ta Soy explains to us that Angkar has need of their services. They come to find them in the evening, and that is the last we see of them. Terror reigns again.

I carry on threshing the rice. The *nearadey* have regrouped the rice stocks of the five villages of the *sahakâr*, and the work all takes place in a single factory adjacent to Ta Soy's house, under the direction of Mme Mao, wife of the storekeeper Ta Suong. We are still as badly fed, but I can manage to make ends meet with the little bit of rice I steal from work every day. Moreover, all the women assigned to threshing do the same without a qualm; it's too tempting when we work all day with this precious commodity and then in the evening, after the daily grind, have nothing but a ladle of soup … Angkar has turned us into thieves; under the old regime, rotten and corrupt, we were honest citizens!

This is how we carry out our larceny. We always operate when Mme Mao isn't there. We put one or two boxes of rice we have just threshed in a basket, and pile an empty basket on top of the first one. Then, two of us go to get more paddy from the storehouse. Taking turns, one of us will be the look-out, while the other fills up a little cotton bag, attached to her belt, with the rice hidden in the basket. Job done, we go back to work, each of us carrying a basket filled with paddy on our heads. Two other women go to the storehouse in their turn, and so forth until everyone has some. We are a dozen workers threshing thirty sacks weighing a hundred kilos each day; with our system, that's one or two savings that disappear daily from Angkar's stocks.[2]

Once the operation is over though, the bags get in the way, hidden round our waists or outside our trousers under our *sampots* (some make a pocket to get it done more quickly). If we have helped ourselves too early in the morning and the day is long, we hide our booty in the bushes behind the factory. If we're unlucky, some of the roaming *sahakâr* pigs pass by, and then we find our bags empty, or even no bags at all. But sometimes I manage to steal two bags a day, the equivalent of two boxes of rice: what luxury, what bliss!

There's just the two of us in the hut now, my little nephew and me. Now and then, my son comes by to cash in on these 'spoils of war'. Sometimes, after having gulped down his bowl of soup at his camp for *kômars*, he slinks off and passes by the village to fill up on rice.[3] Unfortunately, we have to cook it quickly and in secret. While I cook, Ha keeps

2. One saving corresponds to about 50 boxes.
3. Boys are *kômaras* and girls are *kômareys*

watch under the hut.

From August to October 1977, we are no longer assigned to thresh the rice. Angkar has found a machine at Phnom Leap which will do the work instead. But there is no time for a breather. Ta Suong sends us to Koh Tral, another island, to plant kilometres of corn, manioc, sweet potatoes, sugar cane and other vegetables. Before we start, we have to clear two hectares for the manioc. I like breaking up the lumps of earth because I always find insects or scorpions, which are essential food. Since the threshing came to an end, we miss the rice we used to sneak out in our trousers terribly ...

One day, while clearing, I come across a nest of termites, seething with white larvae. Wracked with hunger, I stick my head in and gobble them up raw. At the time, it's a real treat! But the next morning I itch all over and scratch so much that my face completely swells up. An old woman tells me I should drink a tisane made from cannabis leaves to calm the itching. Not knowing it's a drug, I get some from a lad from Phnom Penh who has two plants' worth. The concoction is miraculous, calming both the itching and hunger pains ... but the next day, I feel an urgent need to have some more. The lad gives me a few more leaves, which I hurriedly cook with my wild spinach. My soup tastes excellent and, after having drunk a bowl of it, I'm no longer hungry and feel rather euphoric! On the third day, the source runs dry. My supplier will only give me leaves on the condition that I give him rice in exchange. Happily his greed stopped me from becoming hooked on cannabis.

On 30 October, during a large education meeting presided

over by Mme Chem – a *nearadey* representing all the women of our *sahakâr* – we learn that the machine from Phnom Leap has run out of diesel and doesn't work any more, and that the local mills will start up again.[4] It's good news for thieves! So on 1 November, I joyfully restart my work, believing that I'll be able to feed myself more easily.

One morning, when a chill north wind is blowing, as can happen in November and December, the cold and the hunger seize control of me. So I get up earlier than usual to make some soup with a couple of handfuls of rice and lots of water. But Ta Li is already doing his rounds with a *schlop*. Silently, without any warning at all, he climbs into my hut – our huts have no doors, anybody can enter anytime – and asks me why I'm cooking so early. Before I even have time to reply, he lifts the lid of my saucepan. My only choice is to say that I was feeling weak and hungry:

"Where's this rice from?"

"Grains my son got in the fields after the harvest."

He says nothing, empties the saucepan of water which he then puts back on the fire. All the liquid evaporates, leaving just a layer of solid cooked rice. Then Ta Li takes me to his brother-in-law Ta Ling and shows him the evidence of my crime, explaining that he found me cooking rice. This is a lie, as he saw that I was making soup, not rice. He says that I stole this rice during the threshing.

The verdict comes quickly. Ta Ling gets up, goes to find a pickaxe, and takes me to the communal vegetable patch where there is still some land to be cleared and dug over, fif-

4. The *nearady* instituted a meeting that took place at Phnom Leap at the end of every month to bring together the whole *sangkat* and review the problems of each village.

teen metres square. He orders me to clear and dig the square during the day. If I don't finish by evening, the area will be doubled. I'm also to be deprived of my two food rations.

I'm not the only one to be punished. An old Chinese lady is already there, like me caught red-handed cooking rice. Her husband is in charge of making fertilizer with dried cow's dung mixed with ashes of burnt rice paddy husks. Every day he collects sacks of husk from the factories to burn them not far from his hut. The workers, in solidarity, sometimes exchange some vegetables or fish, and sometimes a bit of rice. Then he just has to sieve it discreetly to separate the good grain from the shell ... In short, he's the thief, but it's the wife who cooks the rice, and it is she who is punished.

Later in the day, another man joins us in our punishment zone. His wife and children are ill with nutritional oedema and he came to beg for a bit of rice bran from the factory, but Mme Mao refused, and in despair he resolved to take a big risk; he cut some paddy plants from a field that had not yet been harvested ... [5]

I finish my punishment around midnight, by the light of the moon, my hands bleeding. The next day, I go back to work. Nobody says a thing.

Towards the end of December there is another disaster. Angkar allows all the children to return to the village. To celebrate, I want to cook them a bit of rice; it's broad daylight and no one will see the fire. But I haven't taken into consideration Ta Ling's wife, who, with her cook, chooses this moment to visit each hut on the pretext of looking for

---

5. Since the arrival of the *nearady* even gathering the grains or sheaves is forbidden. Some people steal whole sacks of paddy which they grind secretly in the forest.

pots for the communal kitchen. Warned at the last minute by Ha, who's on guard but doesn't see her approaching from behind, I hurry to hide the still-hot saucepan of rice in a sack of clothes. But the chief's wife has come to search. She goes through everything, emptying all the sacks, including those with clothes in them. Flashing a triumphant smirk, the bitch picks up the saucepan and takes it off to her husband without a word. My lapse is serious, as last time I promised I wouldn't do it again.

I'm immediately summoned to Ta Ling, who gives me an icy stare, totally devoid of mercy. Once more, he puts a pickaxe in my hands. This time it is not fifteen by fifteen metres that I have to clear, but twice that. The sun is already high; I've the rest of the day and all night to complete the task. Fortunately, in the meantime Jean-Jacques arrives. I haven't had anything to eat, so he brings me a couple of handfuls of paddy that he has collected and cooked. Then, as my hands are starting to bleed once more, he helps me a bit, before he returns to his camp at sunset. I finish the chore at three in the morning, as the cock crows … If it had been any later, my punishment would have been doubled.

My workmates aren't happy and rebuke me for having got into this mess. From the start we've all agreed that if a girl gets caught, there's no way she'd ever tell on her neighbour; instead she'd take the whole blame herself. All the same, in the long run, everybody risks being suspected of embezzling the factory's stock.

When Ta Ling sees that nothing will stop the theft of rice or rice paddy from the fields, he ends up placing a gang of *schlops* at the entrance to the village, whose job is to frisk all the workers, harvesters, fishermen and children coming back from work. We all realise that it will become increasingly difficult to take rice on the quiet, especially as the storekeeper, rightly suspicious, takes part in the operation.

One of my colleagues, who's as stubborn as a mule, takes a chance despite everything by hiding some rice in the pocket on the outside of her pants. But they notice her odd walk and she is arrested and searched. The *schlops* find her trove and its treasure in no time. Her punishment is hard; she has to thresh two sacks of paddy a day, by herself, for five days. The pestle on the machine needs the strength of at least two people to lift it ...

When my colleague has done her time, Mme Mao gathers us together: "Dear comrades, don't be corrupt any longer, try to become honest again, better yourselves. Be sure to be frank with Angkar. If you see anyone doing something bad, don't hesitate to tell me!"

In short, she wants us to denounce each other. We can't help sniggering, as whilst she lectures us, we already have our precious cargo around our waists. That particular day, we were lucky enough to get back without incident, without passing a single policeman. Where have they gone? The regime is mystifying ...

10/ Chaos

At the end of January 1978, we are told that the temperamental Phnom Leap threshing machine is working again and that the little factories in the surrounding *sahakârs* are to close. This turn of events isn't good for the women, particularly the wives of traitors ... since anyone whose husband was taken to the re-education camps will not stay idle for long. We are the first to be sent to O'Leap and Lahal Souy to build dykes. Potentially guilty ourselves, we are watched while we work and they keep an eye on our slightest movements.

So what is this dam-building project, that Ta Soy announced the day he was inaugurated as chief? Important foreign engineers, here to advise on irrigation matters, have decreed that by carrying water all over the place, these dykes will allow the land to yield as much as three times more per year, thereby tripling production. "We must battle on comrades! With these dykes and canals we shall be able to make more land prosper and you'll be able to eat three times a day." So the refugees are to work non-stop day and night to finish the work before the rainy season begins. Even the smallest patch of earth will be turned into a paddy field ... Alas, our efforts will come to nothing and will result in catastrophe. As soon as the rains start, everything will be flooded! Today, I have concluded that the engineers were either incompetent, or they knew very well that these dykes would flood the region and thus drown all the people already condemned by the Khmer Rouge.

In the meantime, I'm on the list of those leaving for the titanic building site at O'Leap. This work would have been both bearable and conceivable if we had been in good health, but not in the physical condition we were at that time. I see that there might be a chance to get out of it, as the threshing machine at Phnom Leap is up to its old tricks and breaks down yet again because of the lack of fuel – the little local production factories must be urgently restarted … Those rare women who still have a husband stay in the village and get on with threshing the rice. Mme Mao thinks she is short-handed and tries to call me up for this task, but it's too late, I'm already enlisted in the dyke construction team, under the direction of the pitiless Ta Soy … Fate certainly has it in for me.

My new work really is hard labour. We have to hack away continually at the solid clay soil under a blazing sun. There's no shade, and no river nearby. To quench our thirst, we only have stagnant water from the paddy fields. The hours of 'work' are always the same; from five to eleven in the morning and from half past eleven until five in the afternoon without a break. The pause for the ladle of soup only lasts half an hour. We don't return to Loti at nightfall, but camp where we are. Conditions are worse than in the village, but above all one mustn't complain.

The dyke is starting to take shape when one evening, during a brainwashing meeting, Ta Soy brings the whole camp together and tells us abruptly that Angkar has decided that the dyke we are digging will be christened *Tonoup Mimai*, the 'Widows' Dyke'. On hearing this ominous name, all the women present, including myself, look at each other in silence for a few moments, understanding, without wanting to understand and without saying a word. At this very moment, a trigger goes off in my head, though deadened by hardship, tiredness and exhaustion. A shiver of fear ripples through my body; now, two and a half years since Seng left, I officially learn that it's ages since he was murdered! How can our torturers be so perverse, so cruel, to inflict such wickedness on us? Why didn't they tell us honestly what had become of our husbands? Why do they need to play cat-and-mouse with us? The last straw of this hypocrisy is that, as we are forbidden to show our emotions in any way, we must clap at the end of Ta Soy's speech to express our approval of his announcement!

With heavy hearts, we walk back silently to the camp, and try to behave as though nothing had happened. The faint hope I'd cherished that I would see Seng alive again is now definitively swept away. Now an indescribable mental fatigue is added to my physical exhaustion, but it's strictly forbidden to stop working or we will be immediately accused of sabotage, hypochondria, or being 'useless mouths'. So the next day, and those that follow, I go back to the construction site to finish my share of the daily hard labour.

The 'Widows' Dyke' must be two kilometres long, three metres wide and four metres high. The earth that has to be dug is heavy clay; we must turn it over, then gather it up and carry it to the site of the dyke in two wicker baskets suspended from bamboo poles balanced across our shoulders. At first, we unload our cargo at ground level without climbing, but as the work progresses, we have to climb up two metres, then three, then four, to unload the earth from our baskets, each of which weighs around ten kilos. After a few of these trips, the little hill seems a mountain up which my legs can barely carry me!

I count each day that passes. I obviously no longer believe in Angkar's promises since its victory over the Khmer imperialists, but hope only for help from the outside! My mind rings with so many unanswered questions ... is there, somewhere in the world, someone who knows what we are going through? Does anyone know what we have to put up with? Apart from those allies who are our executioner's accomplices, is France doing anything to rescue her nationals trapped in this torture? Does she know where I am? Are there other French citizens in this hell?

Exhausted after a week of this treatment, I get ill again. I don't have the strength to lift my pick, let alone bend down to put the yoke on my shoulders. But that heartless Ta Soy doesn't want to know. He never stops badgering me, saying that I only fake illness to return to the village, and leaves me to carry on labouring. I drag myself around the site, where I can barely manage to cart four to six baskets of earth a morning. I'm at the end of my tether, so one day, instead of going to work, I take a risk and go to the village in the hope of finding a little rice bran from the mill and salt, both of which are in cruelly short supply at O'Leap. I wouldn't have been missed if the Khmer Rouge cook who spotted me at the entrance to the village hadn't denounced me. On my return in the afternoon, Ta Soy lectures me severely and threatens me with a one-way trip to the west, all the while calling me a hopeless imperialist. At the meeting that evening I have to criticise myself in front of all the other women and promise not to do it any more: "Comrades, today I committed a serious crime against Angkar. I didn't go to work. Instead I went to Loti and stole some rice bran and salt. I know that this is wrong, against Angkar's commandments, but I promise not to do it anymore and if I should err again you can punish me ..." This is completely untrue, as I didn't steal, I begged for the rice and salt, but this is the way to handle it; if you have done wrong, the best thing is to make an immediate *mea culpa* in public, admitting to crimes you haven't committed, without actually saying that you have been driven to it by hunger. This way you can escape the worst.

After this, begging in the village is totally out of the question. So I use the half-hour break to gather paddy from the paddy fields not far from the site of the dyke. Each time, I pick up two or three handfuls which I carefully put on one side. When I have enough to fill a bowl, I pound it by making a hole in the ground. Sieved, a bowl of paddy can yield about three handfuls of rice, which is better than nothing. To cook it secretly without a saucepan, I wrap the grain in a wet cloth which I bury a few centimetres deep into the soil and I light a little fire with some branches on top of the hole that is covered in earth.

Forcibly underfed and slaving from seven in the morning to five in the afternoon under a blinding sun, I end up suffering from *hemeralopia* (problems with night vision) for several weeks – the Cambodians call it 'the chicken sickness'. In the evening, from sunset onwards, I become blind. There's a sort of white veil in front of my eyes, which disappears in the morning when the sun returns.

There's a full moon, and to get the work on the infamous 'Widows' Dyke' moving as fast as possible, Ta Soy makes us work at night. With my eye problems I'm completely incapable of getting to the building site, but he claims that I'm still feigning illness so that I can shirk my obligations. After two days, to make sure, he asks one of the *yautheas* to carry out a test. The latter comes up to me unannounced and acts as if he is punching me right in the face, but when his fist comes in front of my face I neither flinch nor blink (it's the other women who tell me this, I didn't see a thing). At last they are convinced that I'm really unwell and I'm let off night work.

One day when Ta Soy has had a pig killed for the workers at the camp, the wife of the cook who's the sneak, aware of my eyesight problems, takes pity on me and secretly slips me a piece of liver, telling me to eat it in seven goes (seven is a lucky number for Buddhist believers). I follow her advice and grill this precious piece of liver and cut it into seven tiny slices that I savour. After three days my eyesight returns to normal. Some years later I work out that these problems must have been caused by a vitamin A deficiency, which I overcame by eating the liver.

The days and nights pass and our boss thinks that the work isn't moving fast enough. So he decides to assign us all a quota of clearing four cubic metres of soil a day. If you're too weak, you can share your quota with someone else, but then the amount is doubled!

Those who finish ahead of time – that is those who are still somewhat fit – are allowed to go. They take advantage of this to hunt for a bit of food, fish, gather paddy or pick water plants. In my condition, I have to team up with a girl whose physical state is more or less similar to mine, and we barely finish our work in the allotted time given to us. The result is no fish, no paddy, only the obsessive fear of seeing our ration of rice soup diminish. At this point, I can't get any thinner; I'm just skin and bone. I feel completely empty and I start to feel oppressive, sharp pains in my chest.

During my time at O'Leap, I share a tent with a Chinese woman called Hong. Until now she has managed to hide her real profession from the Khmer Rouge (she was a nurse in the Chinese hospital at Phnom Penh). She has also kept her acupuncture needles, which are a wonderful help when we have migraines, toothache or colic. Her needles perform miracles, even if once, when she was trying to alleviate a compatriot's bad headache, she jabbed in the wrong place and nearly sent her to the next world ...

From mid-February to the beginning of April, we, the widows of the *sangkat* of Phnom Leap, have only built about a kilometre and a half of the 'Widows' Dyke'. Suddenly, for some obscure reason I don't know, we are made to pack up our camp and are sent to a village called Lahal Souy, six kilometres to the south, where the grass stands two metres tall, as far as the eye can see. Here we make our new camp.

The level of the land is lower than that at O'Leap, and yet we get orders to build a dyke six metres high, even higher than the last one. At first the construction is extremely laborious. First, we have to clear the land. The earth is hard, the sun beats down on us, my constantly empty stomach cries out for food and the first rains wash away the earth we have piled up for the base of the dyke. So after each rainstorm we must re-do the previous days' work. As for our diet, it doesn't get any better.

Every morning, when I wake and think of the drudgery that awaits me, I'm in despair. I pray to the Good Lord to intervene so that this endless suffering comes to an end, but it seems as if He is too busy elsewhere and He doesn't hear me.

My only consolation, in this lost corner at the end of the world, is that there are edible water plants and fieldmice. In places, this weed grows for miles. It's extremely sought after, as it fills you up, but it upsets your insides if that's all you eat.

One day, extraordinarily, I finish digging my quota of earth before five o'clock and go to harvest some. About fifty metres away, in the field next to us, a young Cambodian girl just like me is picking these water creepers and putting them in a metal mess tin. Suddenly, the sky grows dark with big black clouds and a violent storm breaks. But we both carry on picking, despite the torrential downpour. I tremble with cold and fear but hunger still drives reason away. Suddenly a deafening noise crashes around my head and there is a blinding flash of light in the storm-darkened field. Panicked, I look around for the other girl and see only an inert, black, huddled heap. She's dead, struck by lightning. Horrified, I run to the camp to get help. But at the camp another horrible surprise awaits me; half of our shelter is on the ground and our soaked things are scattered everywhere. This tragedy frightens me so much that even today I can't take violent thunderstorms and lightning.

This place is teeming with a second treasure, rats and

fieldmice. You only need to recognise their holes. When you've caught sight of one, you just need to dig down twenty to thirty centimetres and you find the whole nest. For starving people like us, these little animals are a luxurious platter that can be bartered for the price of gold.

Near our construction site, as well as rats you can find big black snails, little crabs and lots of mussels in the stagnant marshy pools, although the collection of these is complicated by the horrible leeches ... As we squat in the water right up to the neck to fumble in the muddy bottom where the mussels live, it's important to tie up the ends of our trousers, our shirts at the waist and sleeves and neck, if we want to stop these horrible things latching onto our bodies. Despite these precautions, I come out one day with four huge and horrible leeches wound around my neck and decide that I'll pass on the mussels ...

I am tormented, tortured, by hunger – yes, I call this a slow-burning torture, a death sentence by degrees, because who could ever have imagined that men, such as these Khmer Rouge, could be perverted enough to watch us die of hunger without so much as lifting a little finger?

I have no self-respect left and go regularly to beg the cook for a bit of burnt rice from the bottom of the pan, or some of the rice water that she usually throws out the moment it's boiled or puts on one side for Angkar's pigs. Most of the time, I'm snubbed, called all sorts of names, but who cares, my hunger has desensitised me ... and just the sight of the rice water makes me drool. At this stage, a human being has no dignity. What pride can be left in me when I go as far as to compete with animals for their food?

Since Angkar sent me to work on the dams, I haven't seen Jean-Jacques, who is still assigned to Krasang-ot-Krop, nor my little nephew in the village. In April 1978, I spend the 'feast' of Chaul Chhnam without the children, in the camp at Lahal Souy. Three days of 'holiday', during which we don't work, but we have to get up at dawn all the same to go to these infamous brain-washing meetings. Physically it's a rest time, but Angkar wants to morally rearm us. Moral training must continue ...

The first morning, we are summoned at six to a wasteland where an altar and a ceremonial coffin have been set up. A pair of young Khmer Rouge, all in black, flank the coffin, facing the flag of liberated Kampuchea which flies at half-mast. We all sit in rows on the ground. The officials arrive at seven, as well as all the authorities from the work camps in the neighbourhood. The *canak dambaung* presides over the ceremony; the flag is saluted to the sound of the national anthem on a radio, which is followed by an extremely long and boring speech from Phnom Penh by I don't know whom, and of which I understand nothing, as my mind travels a thousand miles away. They can keep us physically imprisoned, but they cannot lock up our minds.

Then the *canak dambaung* starts his speech. He repeats all the usual orders which we know by heart before abruptly changing the subject; he talks about battles going on against the Vietnamese ... battles, what battles? At these words, I jolt awake and emerge from my daydream with a tiny flicker of hope: "Could these be the saviours we have been waiting for for three years? Might our living hell soon be coming to its end?" The *canak dambaung* continues his speech, and sets about describing the enemy, the Vietnamese, called

Vietcong; they have black teeth and are cannibals, they eat their victims! I'm not fooled by these alarmist statements as I know the Vietnamese, but we all pretend to approve and thank him for warning us. We are set free at the end of his sermon; it must be around eleven o'clock.

For the next two days we are offered up the same ceremony. Later on in the afternoon of the third day, Ta Soy calls us together to tell us not to stray too far from our camp, because, he says, there are Vietcong cannibals in the neighbourhood. Then he questions us to see if we have fully understood the speech from Phnom Penh and if we have any opinions we would like to express on this topic. Total silence. Either nobody dares to speak, with good reason, or, like me, nobody has taken on board a single word. So the session is rapidly brought to an end and we can all go our separate ways to chase after something to eat, our daily obsession.

We were a little more spoilt during those three days; a pig and an ox were killed for around a hundred people and they gave us palm sugar and a sugary dessert made from gluey rice and manioc. Alas the unexpected supplement was short-lived, as after the three days of feasting, it's back to the daily grind and once more we must tighten our belts. Brain-washing meetings, for what they call 'education', and self-criticism sessions flourish aplenty. We have the right to criticize our neighbours, and even, from now on, the president of the *sahakâr* or the village chief.

What a shambles! I start to ask myself what lies behind these incoherent threats, and what's really going on in Phnom Penh and in the rest of the country … Might a miracle be about to happen? Has the Good Lord finally heard my prayers? For three and a half years, my body has suffered so much, worn out by hard labour, starvation and various sicknesses. Still, every time the instructions change, my spirit can't help hoping that eventually someone will come to our aid, deliver us from this hell, and that our martyrdom will end ... unless we die first. Death would be a liberation.

The dyke at Lahal Souy isn't getting any higher. One fine May morning in 1978, marvels from another world appear, three tractors which, in three days, speed up the work that would have taken months for us to complete. We, the widows, are consequently sent back to O'Leap to get on with transplanting work and the construction of little dykes separating the paddy fields. Younger people, who are still just about sturdy enough, replace us at Lahal Souy.

We are put into teams of ten to uproot and replant the rice. But to construct the thirty-centimetre-high and twenty-centimetre-wide dykes that surround the fields, we each have to build ten metres a day. This work soon proves to be exhausting and we need to eat more, but the ration is cut yet again.

By a stroke of luck, the cooks at O'Leap are new. They don't know us. To take the edge off our hunger a little bit, my friend Hong (the nurse) and I pretend we are sisters-in-law. When the rice soup is distributed, I go first to get mine and hers (that of my so-called relative), then she goes to fetch hers. This way we get three rations for two, which is still something.

Unfortunately, we don't get away with this trick for very long. The team in charge, swept up in a wind of panic, is replaced again. Ta Soy puts the village chief, Ta Ling, in charge, and he puts together teams of twenty people, with a head in charge of each one responsible for everything, including the distribution of food. The latter is expected to know, and so recognize, his twenty subordinates, at work as well as mealtimes … No more trickery is possible. We have four teams of women and one of men in our camp.

In June 1978, I begin to swell, and my legs blow up once more. Carting several cubic metres of earth a day becomes an abominable suffering. I can barely put one foot in front of the other, but I have to force myself to drag my body around the construction site for fear of losing my rations.

Then, inexplicably and unexpectedly, my wretched lot is softened by a new regulation; family groups are now acceptable … My son hears by word of mouth that I'm working very hard and with great difficulty building the little dykes. So, he asks his team leader for permission to change work camps so that he can be closer to me. They agree, and so he comes to join me in my nightmarish existence. His presence is a great comfort to me, and his help is welcome. It's a very moving moment when I realize that Angkar has not managed to completely destroy affection between parents and their children – as far as we are concerned anyway – because despite the hunger and the adult work he has to do, Jean-Jacques never hesitates to help me whenever he can. He, too, pretends to have swallowed all their doctrines in order to stay alive.

Soon after this, my little nephew, Ha, comes to O'Leap too. He's like a skeleton, his body covered in bruises. He tells me how he stole some manioc with some other boys of his age – all only between eight or nine-years old – and that they were caught red-handed and severely punished. Fearing the worst, I try to tell him not to do it again, but to no avail. One morning, at dawn, he disappears with two little Chinese boys, carrying a cotton bag. That evening the three children return laden with food: ears of corn, *prahok*, dried fish, even fresh eggs. Very worried, I ask him where it has all come from. "From Mme Chem's, at Phnom Leap", he answers. I tell him firmly never to go back there, explaining that it is too dangerous and that he is risking his life. But I am only his aunt. I have no power over him. He doesn't obey. Over the following days, he repeats these escapades of petty thieving and ends up never joining his squad, which is charged with collecting cow dung. And then one evening, he doesn't come home.

The next day, when we are all at work, Ta Ling arrives in our camp and announces: "Comrades, yesterday the *yautheas* killed three boys who were stealing from Mme Chem. They were irretrievably disruptive elements; the matter is therefore not to be regretted. These children deserved to die". And, without even asking who the parents of these murdered children are – because he knows – he turns around and leaves, as if nothing has happened.

The other boys' mother and I just look at each other, bereft, but unable to say anything. We know full well that it was our children, but nobody dares speak nor shed a single tear. The loss of Ha affects me deeply, but I can't say anything. I'm only sorry that he didn't listen to me. I had no more influence over him because, for three years, our children have not been our children. The Khmer Rouge have turned them into robots only capable of singing the national anthem and of praising and obeying Angkar. They put it in their heads that we, their parents, are corrupt, rotten and irredeemable ... poor little ones, this is where it leads them. Hunger drives them to suicide.

The reorganisation continues. Does it mean an end to this Calvary? That's an impossible dream! The camps recently set up to build the new dykes are dissolved and the construction workers are sent back to their 'original villages'. The work in the village is organised in a well-defined manner:

- Work Force 1: For those still in good health. Two converted refugees, Ta Vong and Ta Chea, are president and vice-president.

- Work Force 2: Regroups all people of middling strength, not ill but not in best of health either ... Ta Sok (of Kambaul) and Ta Im (of Phnom Leap) are at the head.

- Work Force 3: All the sick and living dead. Under the charge of Ta Doeung (also of Kambaul) and Ta Cheng (former chief of a neighbouring village).

Of course, I'm in the last squad. Of the three crews, only the first, about twenty strong, can plough the paddy fields. Normally, work like this is done by oxen or buffalos. The other two teams are responsible for uprooting the paddy and transplanting it.

I can still just about manage to get from my hut in Loti to the fields. But I sense it's not going to go on much longer. I still know absolutely nothing about what is going on in the rest of the country. And in spite of the changes of place or squad, my life proceeds in a monotonous and despairing fashion. My rice ration is invariably the same, but I want to live, despite everything. I hold out. I want to be able to tell my story. I pray to the Good Lord to let me live a bit longer. Don't they say that it's the worst weeds that have the longest life? I must be one; hope has turned me into a hardy perennial.

I carry on struggling to get hold of something small to supplement my meagre pittance. The harvesters can again gather paddy without being punished. What is going on? Have the *yautheas* received instructions to turn us all into manure? So, ill at ease, I start gathering as my stomach takes priority over fear.

It's towards the end of September when I lose my precious yellow mac that protects me from bad weather and only just miss out on losing my life for good. It happens one day when the weather is truly appalling. It's been bucketing down since morning and the river that surrounds us and separates Loti from the dry land is in full flood. But we must work, as there are still a few hectares of paddy fields to plant out before the end of the rainy season. Overtaken by another bout of malaria, feverish and generally in bad shape, I set off anyway for the fields with the other women before dawn, in the driving rain. My legs tremble feebly, my feet are practically numb; I slip in the darkness on the wet clay soil and fall down every fifty metres. My precious mac protects me as well as it can. We walk on for around two hours; day breaks just as we arrive. It is still raining, but we must go into the water and start work right away, on empty stomachs. At the end of the morning, a radiant hot sun appears, but I'm still shaking with fever. Towards four in the afternoon we've finished and get permission to go back. To return to the village, we must cross the notorious bridge which is only thirty centimetres wide. I'm already in the middle of it when the eight-year-old son of the village chief starts from the other end, without waiting for me to finish crossing. There is only one handrail to hold on to, I hang on to it with my left hand, while with my right arm, I clutch my mac and my basket filled with water plants and crabs gathered in the paddy field. Finding myself face-to-face with this brat, I squeeze to the side to let him pass on the handrail side, but I lose my footing and fall from a height of five metres into the flooding river. I don't know how to swim! I sink right down with my mac and my basket. I swallow a mouthful, saying to myself: "This is it, Denise, your last hour has come this time." Then everything goes black.

When I open my eyes, a refugee from Phnom Penh is holding my head down and shaking me to make me cough up all the water I've swallowed. My saviour saw me fall and dived in at once. I was swept away by the current so he couldn't fish me out until a kilometre downstream. Without him, I'd be dead.

As soon as I feel a bit better, the first thing I look for is my mac … Alas! No more mac! I'm safe and sound but I burst into tears. Between sobs I explain how precious it was to me in rainstorms, especially when I have bouts of malaria. How will I get through the next rainy season?

I don't know yet that there won't be another rainy season in the jungle with the Khmer Rouge – that the Vietnamese are not far away, and that they'll soon bring us help. I don't know, or I don't dare to believe it. Because we have heard so many rumours about the Vietnamese … Every evening during the education meetings, our leaders, consumed by paranoia, endlessly drum it in: "Don't venture far from the village, you'll risk bumping into them," or "They have black teeth and are cannibals". The Khmer Rouge become more and more edgy and there is no leniency for even the pettiest crime. The execution of Ha and his two friends was the first example of this limitless cruelty. Everything is to be feared, because the purification of the 'corrupt' which started in 1975 isn't over yet.

Towards the end of 1978, the *nearadey* launch a new series of summary executions which unsettle us deeply. Anyone caught stealing is killed without further ado. One day, a boy is caught digging up some manioc plants. When Ta Ling is told, he simply says 'to the west', and everyone understands. In the forest to the west, a place has been designated for this dirty work and there are three regular perpetrators: Ta Sok, responsible for the production of fertilizer, and Ta Doeung – both extremely bloodthirsty – as well as a third scoundrel, Ta Chea, a refugee like us, who's totally converted to the Khmer Rouge cause. These gruesome individuals have bloodshot eyes from eating human livers, which they cut out of every condemned victim and eat grilled, with rice wine. They don't hide it – apparently it gives them courage and strength to face the enemy.

We are now in January 1979. Next to the hut that I now share with Jean-Jacques lives a young Chinese girl. Her parents died not so long ago. She's ill with an oedema. One night, hunger drives her to risk stealing some juice from a sugar palm. Anyone can easily climb up these palms, as there is a rattan ladder permanently fixed against the trunk so the precious liquid can be collected. Under the bunches of ripe fruit, there are bamboo pipes through which the juice flows.[1] The young girl swallows a few gulps of the sought-after beverage. But the *yautheas* take her by surprise as they

1. Out of this juice one makes either palm alcohol or palm sugar.

are doing their rounds. To the beat of a drum, she's dragged to the village chief. He leaves her outside all night, trussed up and tied to a tree. The next day the whole village is called together for a meeting in a deserted pagoda, by the road on the mainland. The leaders of several different villages are present. After the usual litany of Angkar's rules of conduct, the girl is brought out in front of the assembly. One of the *yautheas* spells out the charges. They then spread the 'guilty person' on the ground, face up towards the sun. It's midday and the sun beats down fiercely even though there's a light north wind.[2] The young girl is fixed to the ground by stakes attached to her hands and feet. Then, after having coated her face with sugar palm syrup, the *yautheas* put four ants' nests filled with huge red ants around her body and head. The ants start crawling all over her body and face, then they get into her ears and nose. The girl is stung, but despite her cries, her supplications, her promises never to do it again, the *yautheas* are stony-faced, and we, miserable and power-less, are forced to witness this scene unable to intervene. We are told that such a severe punishment will be a lesson to anyone who's still tempted to steal. After an hour the girl is at last freed. We try to help her get back to the island, because she can hardly see and has great difficulty standing up. The next day, I call in to see how she is. The poor girl can no longer move, her face is completely swollen up. She's blind. If only we had any remedies to help her. A little later she will die as a result of the torture, and on the very day the Vietnamese arrive, the day we are liberated. How can fate be so cruel! In the ensuing rush and panic to evacuate, nobody

2. We haven't had watches or calendars for a long time. For the time, the sun is our guide. For the days, the moon serves as a reference; every new moon signifies that a month has gone past.

will bury her, and her body will be left in the hut.

On 8 or 9 January 1979, if I remember rightly, it seems as if our Calvary might be coming to an end. I have strangulating pains which have crushed my chest since the work on the dykes. I have more and more trouble breathing and feel completely used up, and it's come to the point where I can no longer fetch a bucket of water for my vegetable plot. If nothing happens, I'll soon be in the next world. At the end of my tether, I end up spending most of my time in bed and, oddly, nobody comes to stop me.

One morning, as my legs have swollen up again, I drag myself along to Mme Khom, the wife of the president of the *sahakâr*, to beg for a little palm sugar. On arriving in front of her hut, I can see that something very serious is going on, though I don't quite know what – all the *nearadey* of the *sahakâr* are gathered at Ta Soy's, armed to the teeth. Their faces are grim and they seem anxious. Some women are hastily sewing rucksacks and bags together from skins, which they fill with rice. Recently the factories have been threshing fifty sacks of paddy a day. The men, sitting in a circle on the ground, talk quietly. Nobody notices me, so I quietly turn around and hurry back home. My poor befuddled head starts to swirl with questions; might we soon be freed? Do they have orders to kill us all? At sunset we'll know the answer.

Once they've loaded up any old how, with the luggage, sacks of rice, salt and dried fish, men, women and children, they all decamp northwards, with no explanation, not a single goodbye. Knowing them as we do, we are not very surprised by this omission.

So the rats have left the sinking ship, abandoning us to our sad fate. In less time than it takes to say it, everything is looted: fields of sugar cane, stores of rice, sugar and salt. The village chief's pigs are killed, everywhere is stripped bare. For us, who have nearly died of hunger for four years, it's the right outcome, a just revenge. I'm happy and relieved to feel that our living-death is at an end, but at the same time I'm very concerned. I ask myself what on earth is going to become of us. For now, my son and I are reunited and that's the most important thing. Tomorrow is another day.

11/ The Road to Freedom

The next day, refugees come from neighbouring villages and camps bringing us fresh news. The Vietnamese have taken Phnom Leap and the village was emptied of its inhabitants. This explains our torturer's speedy departure.

Should we stay; or should we go? For twenty-four hours, I am torn by the same dilemma just as I was four years ago, in April 1975. What will become of us if we stay? What will we find outside if we do leave this accursed place? Some 'old' Cambodians, who were *nearadey* partisans, are still here and try to detain us: "Where would you go? Who's asking you to leave? Don't you know that death is waiting for you at the end of that road?" In fact, the truth is we don't have much rice, no means of transport (not even an ox-cart,) and the nearest big town, Siem Reap, is sixty kilometres from Loti.

We don't know anything about what is going on outside the village, and even if we have nothing left to lose and our lives are already in a sorry mess, we're afraid. Refugees arriving from neighbouring camps tell us that, in some villages, the *nearadey* are slitting throats and hacking people to death, to make sure that there won't be a single witness left. I remember that, under the pretext of making a reservoir to irrigate the paddy fields, the Loti chiefs made us dig a long ditch, which, they said, was to gather rainwater. In reality, we were digging our own grave. And, then when the moment came, they would have massacred us all and tossed our bodies into the mass grave! I still shiver with horror at the thought of it. Happily in our village they didn't have time to complete their inhuman task before fleeing. But where should we go?

Ta Chea, the Phnom Penh traitor, when he sees me getting ready to leave, tries to dissuade me: "You, *yé ponso*, you'll die on the way. Stay here and wait till someone comes to save you." But I don't trust him anymore. It may seem suicidal to go but whatever I do, I'm likely to die, I have no choice. As regards dying, I would prefer my old bones to be buried somewhere else than in this accursed forest.

I don't leave the village until three days later. Three days during which, left to ourselves, we don't hesitate to pounce on the manioc fields, the vegetables in the communal garden, in short, everything that the butchers left behind in their hasty departure is now ours. There are also two oxen, which the few men, who escaped the purges, and the young boys, slaughter and share out. Two days later, how unbelievably blissful it is to see Jean-Jacques come home his arms laden with good, fresh, red meat, the like of which we haven't seen for an eternity. Of course I'm ill and feeble, but I'm happy, my son is still here with me, skeletal, but a survivor and now we are eating solid hot rice with good beef, grilled and salted as we want it. Another bad dream? I pinch myself to make sure. To think that around a week ago we were sharing a piece of fish the size of a thumb, squabbling over the head because it contains more fat … So the Good Lord has heard my prayers, He has not abandoned us.

Nevertheless my body has trouble digesting this sudden

abundance, which, instead of strengthening me, triggers diarrhoea. I've lost the habit of digesting solid food and my body can't keep in what I eat and this will be the case for several months after we're set free.

The beef is prepared in every possible way: grilled, boiled, in soup with courgettes and manioc, I even salt and dry some for the journey, the road to liberty, just in case. We still don't know what awaits us after Loti. The only thing I can say to reassure us, is to tell Jean-Jacques: "In any case, it can't get any worse …"

Leaving the village presents a new challenge for my emaciated and worn-out body. I can hardly stand up and can only drag myself along on my hind-quarters. Thank goodness for my son, this little man of fourteen and a half. The malnutrition he has suffered from since he was ten has stunted his growth; he barely comes up to my shoulder. But in his head he is already very mature and he helps me as much as he can. It's he who carries all our remaining belongings, basically food and water, on his frail shoulders, on a yoke. He's as haggard as I am, but he holds up and doesn't complain; he has a cast-iron character. At that moment I realise Jean-Jacques has been lucky enough to not catch a serious illness, such as malaria, and is 'only' suffering from nutritional oedema.

It takes us more than two hours to reach the main road, three kilometres from Loti. But the hardest thing lies ahead - crossing the river. When we get to the wooden bridge, I remember my vertiginous fall and am seized by panic. I can't go forward. Jean-Jacques, already on the other side, pleads with me, crying, to make one last effort. So I gather my courage and, without looking down, set off on my hands and knees, praying to the heavens to give me the strength to get to the end. We still have two kilometres to walk before we reach the main road.

Once we reach the road, we hesitate, completely disorientated. Which way should we go? Right? Left? East? West? In the three and a half years that we have been imprisoned '*en liberté*' at Loti, we have lost all sense of direction, besides, in my previous life as a 'corrupted one', I had never heard of Loti and these marshy regions. In all these years of captivity, we were herded to the fields, and never tried to find out our exact location in relation to the capital.

As the sun is beginning to set, and the day is drawing to a close, we decide to spend the night here. Jean-Jacques goes to look for a bit of dead wood and three big stones to make a hearth and then to find some stagnant water in a paddy field to cook the rice and grill a few pieces of dried meat. We're not alone; other refugees, who arrived the previous morning, are also camping beside the road, they don't know where to go either. Fortunately, the weather is fine. In January, it's the best season, the evenings are cool and the days are nice and sunny. After dinner, Jean-Jacques plants four stakes in the ground to attach the mosquito net to, then, we fall asleep quickly on a mat spread out underneath it, our minds at peace with the thought that we are free from our butchers. This time, we are really free.

The next morning, not being woken up by a bell for the first time is blissful! But what sadness and desolation at the sight before us. On the road is a procession of carts, painfully pulled along by oxen that are just skin and bone. They're filled with women, children and old people, all as skeletal as us. They look like a horde of zombies returning to the land of the living. One cart has a bit of room and agrees to take me and my son. All the same, before I get in, I ask the driver, who seems to be in charge of the group, where he's going: "To Phnom Leap". It's a place we know, so with no hesitation, we join them. We spend our second night of the exodus towards real freedom in Phnom Leap. The next day, we continue on foot, with the other refugees, as far as Ta Phon, a few kilometres from Phnom Leap. I crawl more than walk; we don't arrive till after sunset. We spend a third night outside.

From dawn the carts struggle along overloaded with their cargo of the old and sick, while Vietnamese military lorries pass by in the other direction from Siem Reap, taking armed troops to the front where the fighting isn't over yet.

At this point, a Vietnamese soldier, a '*bô-dôi*', gets down from one of the trucks and comes over to our temporary camp to give us some advice in Vietnamese. All the refugees crowd around him for information. I haven't heard Vietnamese, my mother tongue, for an eternity, and I have a little difficulty understanding his northern accent which I'm not used to. All the same I grasp the essentials: "Siem Reap is still quite far from here, don't go on foot, you won't get there in your state. Wait here, the lorries will drop off the soldiers a bit further along. Then, they'll pick you up on the way back."

Reassured and relieved, we stay put. And, indeed, twenty-four hours later, the same lorries reappear, empty, and load up all the living-dead that we've become. Contrary to what the Khmer Rouge tried to have us to believe, these 'cannibal' Vietnamese soldiers are humane and considerate towards us. They don't have black teeth and don't seem to want to eat us. On the contrary, you can see the pity in their faces. I trust them completely. Although it's a short distance to Siem Reap (around sixty kilometres,) it takes more than an hour to get there because the road has been neglected for such a long time and is full of potholes. But the length of the journey is of little importance, because this time, we know our destination, and we're not being transported like cattle. Our rescuers do the best they can for us, the very sick are laid out on military tents. The 'cannibal' soldiers treat us like human beings.

The trucks drop us off in a square in Siem Reap, that's bordered by mango and flame trees. I rediscover this town, once so touristy, where I spent a month, fifteen years ago, when my husband was working with Columbia Films while they made *Lord Jim*.[1] Seng was a stage manager and responsible for the entire crews' canteen. I was pregnant with Jean-Jacques then, and still out of work, so I went with him.

Ah so long ago ... Today the town is completely different, barely recognizable. All the houses, that have been unoccupied for four years, are dilapidated. There are no vehicles, with the exception of the constant to and fro of Vietnamese military lorries. The streets are crawling with refugees pushing carts piled high with everything they've been able to find in the abandoned houses: sacks of rice, bottles of fish sauce, tinned stuff and also anything that the monsters left in their flight.

It takes a bit of time to wake up from the nightmare and realise that we are still alive and free, that the Khmer Rouge are no longer here and that we are returning to a normal

---

1. *Lord Jim* (1965) was an adventure that starred Peter O'Toole and James Mason. It was based on the novel by Joseph Conrad. Due to censorship, the film was never allowed to be shown in Cambodia.

life … well almost. These utopian savages have destroyed everything. No more schools, no more hospitals, no more money, no more businesses, everything has to be rebuilt. How is such lunacy conceivable? And to think that these madmen were advised and assisted in their murderous delirium by the communist Big Brother! And the whole time, the international community didn't so much as lift a finger to stop the massacre! Why? How did the Khmer Rouge keep the country hermetically sealed off from any outside intervention? How did they manage to make the whole world believe that all was well in the country and that its inhabitants were happily living in paradise?

After having overcome all these ordeals, I don't hesitate from saying loudly and clearly that if the Vietnamese had not arrived in time, I would not be in this world to recount the horrors I have seen and endured. I'm not looking to flatter them, I would simply like to thank these soldiers who rescued us from the claws of this murderous regime and saved from certain death the few million Cambodians left alive.

Still drunk with the excitement of this new life and not knowing where to spend the night, we wander wearily through the streets of Siem Reap to find a place to spread out our mat, Jean-Jacques always trotting in front with our meagre bundle on his frail shoulders. Turning into a street, I bump into Hong, the Chinese friend with whom I was teamed up with to build the 'Widows Dyke'. Her husband was murdered when the *nearadey* appeared. Having arrived the day before with her two children, a boy of seven and a girl of five and a half, she had managed to find a place to sleep beneath a house on stilts, and she suggests I join her with my son.

There is still no administrative authority, no land registry, no police to check our identity papers; the refugees squat wherever they can, sometimes pretending to be the owners. We are all left to care for ourselves, while the Vietnamese soldiers, for their part, are snowed under by the continual mass arrival of thousands of refugees each in a worse state than the next.

I park Jean-Jacques in a corner, under the house, and go off to find a bit of food, as we already have nothing left to eat. It's midday, the sky is blue and the sun is shining and there's a light fresh breeze from the north. I'm thirsty and hungry but all the same my legs can just about carry me and I wander, like a lost soul, through the town. The streets are jammed with carts and skeletal survivors. I gather some green fruit from below the tamarind trees.

Wandering about, I bump into a Vietnamese soldier carrying a big bag across his shoulders and armed with a revolver. After I've told him who I am, where I come from and given him a brief account of my last four years in hell, I explain to him that I must absolutely get back to Phnom Penh to ask the French authorities for help. The Vietnamese *bô-dôi*, who is in fact a medical officer, looks me up and down compassionately: "At the moment, the most important thing is to get you better here. Phnom Penh is like a desert, and your country, France, no longer has diplomatic representation here and can't do anything for you right now. Wait here for me. I'll come back." With these words, he melts into the rabble. Without much hope, but too tired to continue my wanderings, I sit in the shade of a tamarind tree and wait for him patiently. In any case I have nothing else to do and no way to cure my hunger. Time passes, and here he is again, as promised, with two big packages: "Here's a little rice and meat, eat them first to regain a bit of strength. Tomorrow morning, present yourself at the camp set up outside the town hospital where you will be given vitamins. Don't hesitate to come to see me if you need any help." And he points out how to find his HQ and Siem Reap Hospital. I thank him warmly and set off with a spring in my step with my wonderful windfall from heaven under my arms that I'll share with my son, Hong and her children. The first packet contains hot rice and the second delicious pieces of meat and grilled, salted fish. Whenever I think of this first meal, I still bless that Vietnamese soldier.

The next morning we all go to the hospital where the *bô-dôi* have set up a sort of tent with tables behind which sit two or three Vietnamese soldiers, who are apparently doctors. They don't examine us and to start with they are happy to hand out multivitamins, rice, sugar, dried fish and a tin of condensed milk for each family. Our saviours recommend we return every two days for supplies. Paradise after hell!

Unfortunately, my body still can't cope with all these wonderful things and after each meal I get diarrhoea. What's more we have neither electricity nor running water in our makeshift camp, there's just a well where we draw some rather questionable water and no toilets. Everyone does their business in or around a dried up pond …

After a week, my strength starts to return thanks to the multivitamins and improved diet. We are not living in the lap of luxury. Our saviours are not rolling in money and they share what they have with us whilst waiting for the eventual arrival of some international aid. I still have swellings and my knees are all puffed up, like cotton wool. I have difficulty standing up. I weigh barely thirty kilos but my swollen stomach, legs and feet make me look like an elephant. The diet of multivitamin meals does Jean-Jacques the world of good. After ten days his oedema has almost disappeared and he looks better. Every day, Dr Mu, the medical officer, visits the various camps in Siem Reap to hand out vitamins, medical care and give a few words of encouragement to the refugees. He comes by to hear our news. This attention boosts our morale and gives us hope. Hong and I wander about town all day long looking for work but the whole place is still in an indescribable chaos and no one knows yet who does what …

The Vietnamese soldiers do all they can to help the living dead who flood in every day, while battles continue in the provinces along the Thai border. Thanks to them, life in the town organises itself little by little. The only hospital reopens to take in the most seriously ill and the wounded, in particular the refugees who have had their throats were cut by the Khmer Rouge, then been left for dead and were finally picked up and brought to Siem Reap by the *bô-dôi*. But there is a serious shortage of doctors and nurses, so, when on one of his visits, Dr Mu finds out that Hong was a nurse, he asks her if she would accept work at the hospital. Without hesitation Hong accepts, and I take advantage of this to offer my services by bluffing a bit about my skills, not wanting to stay idle … And, thus, I'm hired as a nursing auxiliary and Hong as a nurse. This work enables our us all to be cared for a bit better.

The Vietnamese requisition all the empty houses and flats near the hospital to accommodate the new staff. They give Hong and I the first floor of a little house, still standing, but completely abandoned, whose owners have not returned from the exodus. The place is almost empty, there's just a wobbly table, two old chairs and an awful lot of spiders' webs. But for four long years we have had to make do with a mat and a mosquito net on which to rest our skeletal bodies ... In the days that follow, we try to get hold of some beds and kitchen utensils from the unoccupied houses around about. With a few swishes of a broom, we bring life back to this sad place. Since the Khmer Rouge destroyed all the archives in the land registry nobody can yet lay claim to their property. The refugees settle in as best as they can. It's first come, first served!

The hospital buildings are dilapidated and the electricity supply and running water is woefully inadequate. Water for cooking, laundry and washing the sick comes from one well in the hospital courtyard. There is a river a bit further away but it's an extra chore to cart water from there, so we make do with the well. The sick and wounded arrive every day and we must deal with the most urgent cases. We put them in big communal wards which have no beds or mattresses and lay them out on mats on the ground. We help the Vietnamese to dust, wipe away spiders' webs, sweep and wash the floor. The buildings have been abandoned since April 1975.

Hong teaches me how to give intramuscular injections into the arm. It's not that hard. After five or six patients, I get the hang of it. The really badly wounded, like those who have had their throats slashed by the Khmer Rouge, are immediately put in the care of a Vietnamese surgeon who sews up the wounds as best he can. Fortunately, they have basic supplies but they also have to care for their wounded soldiers returning from the front. The latter aren't hospitalised in the same place as the Cambodian refugees but elsewhere. While waiting for help from Vietnam and humanitarian organisations, I learn how sparingly to use 90% alcohol, for injections, and as there are only a few litres left, to sterilize syringes and needles in boiling water and even to sharpen the heads of used needles ...

At first the hospital is run by the Vietnamese who, in record time, manage to assemble a team of Cambodian doctors, to whom they hand over the management after a few months, when everything has been just about reorganised. When the new Cambodian chief doctor takes office, I dislike him on sight, I don't know why ... And it's obvious the feeling is mutual. A few days after his arrival, he changes my job and puts me in charge of washing the invalids' clothing, many of whom are suffering from diarrhoea. Most of the sick have no families, so it's up to us to take care of them completely. Changing those suffering from diarrhoea and washing their clothes is my new job. To do this, I must get water from the well and holding my breath wash the clothes without soap or bleach, using my feet as a scrubbing brush. At midday, I finish my work, worn out and so disgusted by the smell that lingers in my nostrils that I can't swallow anything when I get home. After a week, I begin to waste away again but I carry on, without complaint, doing this filthy job.

One morning, Dr Mu, who has already helped me so much, comes to visit the hospital and finds me drawing water from the well for my washing. Knowing very well that I'm not yet quite recovered, he asks angrily on whose orders I'm doing this work and since when. Then he calls the doctor-in-chief and orders him to discharge me immediately from this job.

The next day my protector finds me work in the hospital pharmacy. I sort through the medicines and instruments and throw away out of date products and classify those which can still be used. It is a painstaking job but less tiring than the previous one. I finish it in just a few days because a lot of products are out of date and there isn't much to salvage, the stock having not been supplied or renewed since the arrival of the Khmer Rouge. Fortunately for me, the Vietnamese have kept control of decision-making in the organisation of this establishment and in the allocation of staff, or I would still be at the mercy of that Khmer doctor.

After the hospital, Dr Mu suggests another occupation; to write down what I have lived through for the last four years! I am not against it but who will feed us if we don't work? "Don't worry about that", he tells me, "Morning, midday and evening you and your son will eat your meals in the *bô-dôi* canteen. We'll give you everything you need to write up your memoirs. Don't try to write a novel, just record what you've seen and lived through, day by day, under the Khmer Rouge regime."

So be it. I accept this task without further discussion, as it will let my son and I have full stomachs. The next day, therefore, I present myself at the Vietnamese HQ A *bô-dôi*, apparently already informed of my mission, puts me in a small peaceful room without asking any questions; it's equipped with a table and chair; he gives me some paper that's turned yellow, carbon paper, pencils and a rubber. Every day, after a copious breakfast with the *bô-dôi*, I set to work, relating, as accurately as I can, these tragic events which overturned my life.

It will take me several weeks to come to the end of my account. It's not an easy task, I don't know where to begin and can only manage a few pages a day. Moreover, putting all this suffering into words is extremely painful …

When I have finished the last sentence, Dr Mu explains that this confession could be used in a possible trial of Pol Pot. I know nothing about the law but have complete confidence in him. I hand over the original manuscript but keep the carbon copy, which I put aside carefully for twenty-five years. It's that copy that I reread and, with hindsight, am correcting today.

Dr Mu then gives me another job which I really enjoy; to translate, from Vietnamese into French, lessons for training nurses drafted by Vietnamese doctors. Because there is such a shortage of hospital staff, as most of them were either massacred or fled the country before the chaos, the Vietnamese doctors are training up Cambodian nurses and paramedics. But the notes are all in Vietnamese and the surviving Khmer trainees are French-speakers. Speaking and reading Vietnamese fluently, I am well-equipped for this task, it's an intellectual exercise that makes a change from digging dykes or making manure!

My health starts to improve. I am so stuffed with vitamins that after about three months I'm almost fully recovered. It's no surprise that I'm capable of eating a whole saucepan of rice at every meal. However, as I still have an oedema, I am put on a salt-free diet. Every morning at breakfast time in the military canteen, I eat with relish a big plateful of rice with fried fish and sugar. At the time this combination of foods seems to me to be absolutely delicious and the Vietnamese soldiers eat mainly fish caught in the river or beef or pork which are still a luxury.

In short, after the hell that I have just left, my happiness is nearly complete. I feel free, liberated, at last. I bury all my sorrows and heartaches deep inside me in order to move on, to try to live normally again, to rebuild all that those monsters have destroyed, in one word to start from scratch ... Thus, little by little, I begin to enjoy life again, thanks to the good care of the Vietnamese doctors.

Of course, all the care our liberators give us isn't wholly disinterested. In me they have certainly secured a prime non-Cambodian witness to support their cause, one which I support without a second thought. If this trial could punish our torturers ...

Today, I'd like to thank from the bottom of my heart those Vietnamese soldiers who arrived just in time to save the few millions of Cambodians who were left. They saved us, my son and me. All the survivors know very well to whom they owe their lives but most do not want to acknowledge it, nobody wants to say out loud what they all think to themselves ... After I left the country, on 15 November 1979, I cannot testify as to what went on but from January to November 1979, between Siem Reap and Phnom Penh, I only met friendly, courteous, humane and helpful *bô-dôi*, who didn't abuse or put any pressure on the survivors that they snatched from the murderous jaws of the Khmer Rouge. I never witnessed so much as a single act of looting or random violence. On the contrary, they did all that was possible to breathe life back into a battered country that had been emptied of everything, that had no economy, schools, elite, or hospitals …

I'm profoundly grateful to Dr Mu, the medical officer who looked after us from the day we arrived in Siem Reap without ever asking anything in return and I have the greatest respect for him. He was friendly and knew how to do everything. I still remember with deep sadness, one day, when I dropped in on him, I found him in tears. He had just learned that his wife, a teacher, and their two little girls back home, had been killed in a Chinese bombardment. This man's pain still stays with me. What bitter injustice and a dismal twist of fate! When he left to save and protect strangers, he lost all his family who were unprotected at home …

Siem Reap. While I translate the first aid manual, Hong continues nursing at the hospital and Jean-Jacques busies himself giving a helping hand to the Vietnamese soldiers. He collects firewood for the communal kitchen, chops it up, goes fishing on the river with the cooks and helps them clean and gut the fish before salting and drying them to conserve them. All this is a lot of work. There are still no fishermen or nets. To catch a large quantity of fish in the shortest amount of time, the soldiers throw hand grenades into the water. This method is certainly not very ecological, but there are thousands of sick who have to be 'fixed up'. The daily catch doesn't last long; it's salted, dried, or grilled, then instantly distributed among the population. Feeding stations are set up in the different neighbourhoods of Siem Reap and everyone has a daily ration of rice, salt, fish, sugar and also, miraculously, condensed milk (one tin per family, per week) and bananas and oranges that have disappeared for so long from circulation … Local currency is not yet reintroduced, so there is no commerce, and everybody continues to live as a co-operative.

During the first two months of our life in Siem Reap, all the basic necessities distributed to survivors come essentially from Vietnamese aid. We haven't yet caught a glimpse of any international aid or a humanitarian organisation. It's only in March that two French journalists, or maybe doctors - I can't remember which - come to visit the hospital to make an official report on the situation. They interview me, take photographs, promise to help me find my brothers and sister in France and to let the French authorities know about me. Since our return to freedom, our future and Jean-Jacques' studies preoccupy me almost obsessively, just like the hunger in the paddy fields … We have lost everything, those most dear to us, our health and our possessions. We haven't even got a penny and must start again from scratch. But we're still alive; we must look to the future … I can't sit back and do nothing. I must continue to fight …

Shortly after my encounter with the French journalists, I meet a well-known Vietnamese author, Mr. Nguyen Khac Vien. He's come to talk to me about my manuscript which will be a witness statement in the criminals' trial. He also assures me that he will get it published in Europe, on one condition that I take out the parts where I recall my husband's communist ideas and his blind faith in the Khmer Rouge leaders. At the time, I agree, without really understanding Mr. Vien's request. The reason for this censorship is plain to me today. He feared that my remarks might too globally condemn communism!

A little later, two Vietnamese journalists come from Ho Chi Minh City to do a story on the state of the country, with the aim of letting the whole world know what has happened. They film and interview me for two days, with the intention of showing it on television. As they don't speak Khmer, it's my job to act as their interpreter and guide and to visit with them all the places the Khmer Rouge penned in the people. This is how I make a harrowing pilgrimage to Loti, our old 'residence'. The huts that sheltered us are still there but they're a bit dilapidated as the forest has begun to retake possession of the spot. I try to find the place where my family are buried but sadly it's all overgrown. Disappointed and unhappy, I go with the visitors to other such camps that I don't know, situated to the north of Siem Reap, not far from the ruins of Angkor.

Gloomy and sorrowful visits, macabre discoveries. I still feel sick when I think of it. In one village, we find dried up wells filled with human bones; further on, a shed surrounded by three huge ditches full of decomposing bodies, bodies burnt with paddy husks to make human fertilizer. Around the ditches, piled and scattered about everywhere are men's, women's and children's clothes, a nauseating and stifling stench of rotting flesh hangs in the air … I am horrified by the sight; for a good ten minutes, I am dumb. Then I start to sob. How they must have suffered, mentally and physically, before ending up in these ditches! I remember with terror the 'reservoirs' that we dug at Loti …

Two camp survivors forced by the Khmer Rouge to make this human fertilizer, while waiting to be massacred in their turn, have stayed on as they in such a state of shock that they could not leave when the Vietnamese arrived. They give us a terrifying account; the *yautheas* brought their victims by the cartload at nightfall; men, women and children. The women and children were then separated from the men, who had to carry sacks of rice husks to the edge of the ditches. Soon after, the women, children and the men from previous contingents were lined up blindfolded around the ditch, then executed by the *yautheas* with axe blows to the scruff of the neck. No guns - ammunition is too expensive for Angkar ... The remaining men had to strip the bodies and throw them into the ditches, scattering paddy husks on each layer; one layer of corpses, one layer of paddy husks and so on until the ditch was full; then they sprayed it with petrol and set it on fire. Twenty-four hours later, they came to gather the ashes to sieve them. The leftover bones, still whole, were ground into powder with a pestle and mortar and the ashes stuffed into jute sacks to be spread out in the paddy fields as fertilizer. These monsters said that it was free fertilizer for Angkar's coffers and ecologically sound. The three existing ditches burned like this without a break. If the Vietnamese had not arrived in time, these two men would have been reduced to ashes. They had just finished the last batch and twenty-four hours later their turn would have come.

In the neighbouring shed, we find the tools for this macabre work: three pestles identical to those used for milling brown rice, sieves, empty jute sacks and empty or half full oil drums and in a corner, sacks filled with ashes. One of the pestles still has bits of bone in it, waiting to be reduced to powder.

Visiting these dreadful places is a terrible Calvary. It is a disturbing shock that upsets me so much I become anorexic.

On returning to Siem Reap, I can't eat for several days and lose weight again. Dr Mu worries about it and not finding anything clinically wrong with me during an examination, gives me some more vitamins. It's crucial that I look better; the Vietnamese authorities are planning to assemble as many witnesses in good condition as possible for the trial of the Khmer Rouge leaders, Pol Pot and Ieng Sary. I have the feeling that I will be asked to appear …

While I wait, life at Siem Reap gets better every day and an increasing number of foreign journalists pour in. One day, a French journalist from Ho Chi Minh City brings me a parcel from an old colleague and friend from the embassy at Phnom Penh, Cécile Benoliel, now at the French consulate in Ho Chi Minh City. It contains toiletries and a few pairs of little knickers, luxuries that I haven't seen in ages, two tins of condensed milk, as well as a little refined white sugar. Accompanying all this is a note of encouragement, telling me not to lose patience or hope. When I recognise the hand-writing and signature of my friend, I burst into tears. Is this because for four years, I have had to suppress all my emotions? Now, I cry over anything, it's enormously comforting to finally be able to show my feelings again.

This undreamed of present makes me very happy and re-assures me as well. Because if Cécile knows where I am, then France too is aware of my existence and will surely make efforts to get us out of this dreadful place quickly. But things aren't that simple. In the chaos that accompanied the return to freedom many identities were stolen. The Ministry of Foreign Affairs has to make enquiries to verify the information that I gave to the journalists. This work takes time. We are in March 1979 and I shall have to wait until November for the matter to be cleared up. A wait of three to six months, for people with comfortable lives, is a normal delay but for me, every day spent in these places of living death feels like a century. I have only one, selfish thought fixed in my head – to leave the land of my birth, the beautiful country of my childhood where there are so many terrible memories, so as to give Jean-Jacques, who is now almost fifteen, a better life and a normal schooling. I can't waste a second ...

Every day, after my translation work at the hospital, I teach Jean-Jacques using some old French primary school books that were found and saved by some hospital workers in an abandoned villa – an elementary maths and reading book – but it's better than nothing. I try to get him back into the swim of things, so he won't be too lost when we leave and return to the sort of life we led before the hell began.

My poor child, who has suffered so much too, and who, for four years, struggled as hard as I did to survive, without asking questions, without reproaches, without crying, without complaining ... I now desire with all my heart that he be happy, that he regains the life of a child of his age. He is the only treasure I have left.

12/ The Trial

At the beginning of April, I am told officially by the Vietnamese that I am invited to be a witness at the trial of the Khmer Rouge that will take place in Phnom Penh, although they can't specify when. I'm delighted because this will allow me to get back to Phnom Penh, where it will surely be easier for me to hurry up the formalities of my departure. I wait for D-Day impatiently. Every morning when I open my eyes, I ask myself the same question: Am I leaving or am I not leaving? Always the same uncertainties. Days, months pass and still nothing. I get a bit riled by the wait. I go and see Dr. Mu almost every day, pressing him with questions, but he himself knows nothing, or doesn't want to say anything. He satisfies himself with repeating endlessly: "I don't know ... Just be prepared!" I've been ready for a month, since the news was announced. A small bundle containing a few clothes and personal effects is already waiting. The thought of this separation saddens my friend Hong, as she knows that she won't see me again. In any case, once I'm in Phnom Penh, returning to Siem Reap will be impossible.

And then one morning in August, forty-eight hours before the trial, a miracle occurs. At daybreak, two *bô-dôi* accompanied by two Vietnamese in plain clothes[1] come to

---

1. I'll later find out that these were Vietnamese police officers.

collect my son and me in a jeep. The week before, the other Cambodian witnesses had already been taken to Phnom Penh by road. At the same time, I'm very emotional and sad to be leaving Hong, who has been like sister to me since our liberation. Hong is very impressed by the soldiers and seems a little unnerved; she asks me if we're really being taken to Phnom Penh. But I'm not worried at all, and I follow them with complete confidence. The jeep sets off for Siem Reap airport where a military helicopter is waiting for us. When I set eyes on the contraption, I'm momentarily frightened as I have never travelled in a plane, let alone a helicopter! We take our places flanked by two bodyguards. I am a little apprehensive, but Jean-Jacques doesn't say a thing. Is he happy to return to Phnom Penh? Is he frightened? I don't know and I'll never know, because he's always kept quiet about his feelings. Even today he still closes off everything about those four hellish years … The flight lasts longer than predicted. Listening to the Vietnamese pilot talking on the radio, I understand that we have got a bit lost and that we're now over the Thai border. I've no idea of the risks were running and let myself be carried along blithely.

An hour later, we arrive safe and sound in Phnom Penh. The helicopter lands smoothly at Pochentong,[2] where an official Vietnamese car is waiting for us. I finally set foot in Phnom Penh, after four years in exile. What emotions flood through me when I see this familiar place! The airport is still there, but in such a state! The runway is riddled with holes made by the rockets launched by the Khmer Rouge before the fall of Lon Nol's regime. The control tower is still standing, but the surrounding buildings are totally dilapidated.

---

2. Phnom Penh's only airport.

Memories beset me, both sweet and sour. Along the road that leads into the capital from Pochentong, the villas of the rich are still there, but completely abandoned. Their owners probably died during the deportation or are exiled in some other paradise.

As we enter the town, I can't hold back the tears. Tears of joy, but above all of sadness. I feel that life is softly turning a page but the stains of these four years of horror, crime and destruction can't be removed. The city is still in a state of indescribable disrepair. Our Vietnamese hosts give us a tour: we pass Phsa Thmey, the big covered market, around which grow the wondrous coconut trees planted by the Khmer Rouge. The surrounding buildings are in a complete state. The Khmer Rouge transformed them into warehouses, thematically storing the furniture and equipment gathered from the capital's houses in each apartment. Whole apartments are filled up to the ceiling with fridges, televisions, irons, kitchen utensils, furniture, beds or sofas. These monsters categorised everything, just like they did with us. The abandoned carcasses of cars, entirely dismantled, are scattered everywhere … it's an unimaginable mess! The Khmer Rouge banned and rejected everything that, according to them, recalled imperialism and came from the corrupt West. And it was in this state of mind that they wanted to found a new nation!

The Vietnamese drop Jean-Jacques and I off at a hotel, which has been requisitioned to house all the witnesses. It's well-equipped and, during the few days of the trial, we take our meals in a sort of canteen. Miraculously, we rediscover electricity and running water, after having been deprived of it for such a long time. Vietnamese lawyers come to assist those who want expert help to write their witness statements in French or English. The Cambodian witnesses can do this in Cambodian if it's easier for them. I ask them how to present my story. They advise me simply to relate what we have lived through and endured.

The trial is held in the Chakdomuk room (reserved under the old regime, for *soirées artistiques*), not far from the royal palace, in the presence of many local and international lawyers. The French press (*FR3* and *L'Humanité*) and other overseas media are present. The trial lasts several days but I'm only called once. My son comes with me – he's a witness but he's not called. It's the first time in my life that I've spoken at a trial; I'm overwhelmed by waves of painful memories and by a terrible desire for punishment and vengeance ...

I begin by giving my identity in the witness box. Then, a Khmer lawyer reads a summary of two or three pages of the text I wrote at Siem Reap. Then I'm questioned. I'm happy to relate the suffering that I've endured for four years, naming all the loved ones I've lost. I finish by begging the court to condemn those responsible. Other witnesses are then called up; Buddhist monks relate how some of them were eliminated because they were judged to be 'useless mouths' or were forced to marry, something they're forbidden to do. Then, Muslims explain how the minority they represent was massacred; how they were forced to eat pork when others were dying of hunger. Then it's the turn of former civil servants and teachers (who escaped execution by concealing their real job) or peasants, all of whom have lost their families. I listen in tears to these testimonials, each one as excruciating as the last and utterly damning of the Khmer Rouge. The witnesses all recount the same mental and physical suffering. In the absence of the accused, Pol Pot and Ieng Sary, the president of the tribunal has appointed two lawyers to defend them. They are both condemned to death in absentia.

Once this ordeal is over, while waiting to find work, Jean-Jacques and I stay a few more days in Phnom Penh. At the trial, I got to know American and French journalists and an attaché from the Russian embassy in Vietnam. I let them know how eager I am to leave this accursed place as soon as possible; I tell them I am waiting desperately for my country, France, to intervene. When he gets back to Vietnam, the Russian diplomat immediately discusses my case with the French Consul General in Ho Chi Minh City and asks him why France is being so slow in getting one of their imprisoned nationals out of Cambodia. As I will learn later, the consul thinks I talk too much and it annoys him. I believe he was not aware of my situation. For him bureaucracy is bureaucracy, and one must know how to wait! The Russian's intervention has an effect all the same, because two weeks later I receive a letter via the international Red Cross from the French ambassador in Hanoi, telling me that the French authorities are dealing with the paperwork needed for my departure and asking me to hold on a little bit longer.

In Phnom Penh, my Vietnamese protectors – the two soldiers and the two police officers who escorted me from Siem Reap – look after me. One day, they suggest we go to see my old apartment ... I accept, in the hope that I'll be able to recover few things. I have no trouble finding the place but my disappointment is immense. The building is still there but all the apartments have been stripped. But in one of the two apartments that my family lived in I find hanging on the wall, as if by a miracle, a picture painted by Seng – a view across the top of the central market. My past surges back brutally and I can't help dissolving into tears. This painting is the only thing I find. Alas, I had to get rid of it when we left Phnom Penh and so I gave it to an old friend of Seng's that I had come across.

Another test awaits me after this tearful pilgrimage. We go to visit a Cambodian school that had been turned into a detention and torture centre by the Khmer Rouge, the Lycée Tuol Sleng. There, I discover the immeasurable horror of the atrocities they committed. In the entrance hall, the Khmer Rouge have piled up the clothes of men, women and children who were imprisoned and murdered. Their photos hang on the surrounding walls. They all have a small sign hanging around their necks with a number on. In vain, I look at each one, in the hope of finding Seng. In another room, a pile of human skulls and bones has been gathered from the communal graves and put here in front of us in memory. Every classroom is divided into several minuscule prison cells: on the walls are manacles and chains, and there is barely enough room for a man to lie down ... Their cruelty even extended to noting the details of the tortures inflicted on the prisoners in registers. You can read, for example, that they burnt the tongue of one man with cigarettes to make him talk, and they removed another man's liver before he died. Diagnosis: "good quality liver". I had always thought that after the Nazis such horrors could never happen again. And to think that later, in France, malicious journalists and anti-Vietnamese have the nerve to claim that Tuol Sleng was just a masquerade, and that it was staged by the pro-Vietnamese regime. How can anyone be so stupid?

When we leave the school, I throw up my lunch.[3]

A few days later, the Vietnamese police officer informs me that they've found me a job at the Ministry of Health while I'm waiting to leave. It is based in the former Comin Khmer company premises, where I once worked ... In return, I'll be allowed to stay in an apartment in a building that has been requisitioned for ministry personnel, and we'll have access to the communal canteen where we'll be served morning, midday and evening, with rice and *prahok* (the dish that I dreamt about at night when hunger kept me awake), or banana trunk soup. We are free to eat there or to take our ration home. Since we don't own any kitchen utensils, we can't do any cooking yet. Before Cambodia regains a normal life culturally, economically, medically, socially and health-wise, and while waiting for the humanitarian and international aid to arrive, the Vietnamese continue to do their best to provide the basic necessities for the survivors. The local authorities redistribute the furniture, mats, saucepans and so forth that they've salvaged from the apartments our 'guardians' turned into warehouses four years ago, when they told

---

3. In July 2007, Kaing Guek Eav, the head of Tuol Sleng, became the first member of the Khmer Rouge to be charged with crimes against humanity by a UN-backed tribunal in Cambodia. Tuol Sleng was known by the regime as S-21. When the Khmer Rouge were ousted from power and driven into the jungles of north-western Cambodia by the invading Vietnamese army, Kaing Guek Eav, known as 'Comrade Duch', disappeared like most other senior figures. Using various aliases, he lived in a Khmer Rouge stronghold until 1999 when he was discovered by journalists. By that time he had ended his association with the regime, converted to Christianity and was working as a volunteer for the charities World Vision and the American Refugee Committee. In July 2007 Duch was formally charged with crimes against humanity and detained by Cambodia's United Nations-backed Cambodia Tribunal. On 20 November 2007 the tribunal began hearing Duch's appeal against his provisional detention.

us to leave without worrying as they would look after our houses …

Jean-Jacques, who's almost fifteen and considered to be an adult, is offered a job by the ministry as well, of which he's very proud. Bare-chested and barefoot, he is dressed only in shorts and carries a gun. He's employed as a security guard in front of the ministry.

For my part, I become the Minister of Health's interpreter; he's a Khmer krom and … a Khmer Rouge from the pro-Vietnamese faction.[4] The Minister understands Vietnamese better than Cambodian; as I speak Vietnamese, English, French and Khmer, I gradually become his 'right hand man', which makes his *chef de cabinet*, an extremely erudite Cambodian, rather jealous. I need new clothes for work. The Minister gives me the name of a dressmaker, whose job it is to kit out all the personnel using material that comes from Vietnam. I am made two *sampots* of purple cloth and two shirts with pink and white stripes. They're a lot more cheerful than the black clothes forced on us by Angkar. I'm even entitled to a pair of completely new sandals.

The minister and I get into the habit of talking to each other in Vietnamese. So when the new pro-Vietnamese Prime Minister receives a delegation of Oxfam doctors – which sends the government a boatload of medical equipment, medication and powdered milk – I translate directly

---

4. The Khmer kroms are Khmers who live along the Khmer-Vietnam frontier, and more often than not they speak Vietnamese rather than Khmer. One day, some Cuban journalists interviewing the Minister in my presence said: "Minister, as a former Khmer Rouge you also have blood on your hands!" The Minister justified himself by saying that the pro-Vietnamese Khmer Rouge had quickly come out against the policy of purges and mass executions adopted by the pro-Chinese Khmer Rouge. That was the beginning of the schism between the two factions.

into Vietnamese instead of translating the discussion with the British visitors into Khmer. The Prime Minister apparently understands without any difficulty. But the *chef de cabinet* is not happy and asks me later why I insist on not speaking Khmer in the Minister's presence.

The Minister of Health is very kind to me and appreciates my interest in the work I've been given. One day, he advises me to read Lenin's biography in Vietnamese, a big book that has pride of place in his library and which he lends me. I have other things to do, but so as not to irritate him I let him lend it to me, though I'll give it back before leaving without even having opened it! Every evening after work, I continue to make Jean-Jacques work through the school textbooks that I brought with me. Day by day I am thrilled to see that he is making enormous progress in reading. In maths, I can only teach him multiplication tables, basic calculations and a few geometric formulas. Routine slowly takes hold in our new life, but it's a routine markedly more pleasant than the hell we have known …

The minister quickly becomes aware of my desire to leave Cambodia but, aware of the difficulties I'll encounter, he suggests that I stay at the ministry to continue my mission. Some doctors from *Secours Populaire*, a humanitarian aid agency linked to the French Communist Party who arrive at more or less the same time as Oxfam, also ask me to work for them. But none of this dissuades me from my goal of leaving the country. My priority is Jean-Jacques – his studies, his future – and for that I am ready to face anything to start a second life. There is nothing to keep me in Cambodia. I have to rebuild my life, as the Khmers have to rebuild their country. It will be as enormous a task for me as it is for them …

So I continue my preparations for departure to France. I try to be patient and persevere. Life at the ministry isn't dull – we begin to receive a lot of visitors: journalists, doctors and representatives of international humanitarian organisations such as the International Committee of the Red Cross (ICRC).

The international aid that starts to arrive (medicines, powdered milk, sugar and medical equipment) brings a physical and mental comfort to a deadened and resigned people. A few Cambodian doctors who escaped the genocide have managed, with the help of Vietnamese doctors, Oxfam and the *Secours Populaire*, to reopen the Faculty of Medicine so they can rapidly train the doctors and nurses that the country so desperately needs. They have to get the two big hospitals in Phnom Penh up and running, the Calmette and the Chinese Hospital, as well as a few paediatric centres.

The country opens its doors to foreigners but there is still an atmosphere of distrust and of suspicion. The Minister of Foreign Affairs doesn't hesitate to provide guides to visitors, apparently as interpreters but in fact to spy on them. Once, I had the opportunity, along with two colleagues from the Ministry of Foreign Affairs, to accompany two Oxfam doctors to Sihanoukville to receive a cargo of medicine and powdered milk. It's an opportunity for me to see again the beautiful seaside resort that was so popular with Cambodians until 1970. Of course, all the gorgeous villas, the former holiday homes of the rich of Phnom Penh, are broken down and looted. The sand on the beach is white but the forest has reclaimed a large part of the town and there is a lot of work to be done … The government has requisitioned and done up the villa of Prince Norodom Sihanouk to accommodate foreign visitors, and it's there that we spend the night before we take delivery of the Oxfam aid the following day. All these contacts with foreigners reassure me.

I take part in the meetings with interest, and take my role of interpreter very seriously. Every time a French journalist visits the ministry, I give him a letter addressed to the Minister of Foreign Affairs in Paris, imploring him to speed up my case … I don't let a single opportunity pass me by.

I get to know Alain Ruscio, a correspondent for *L'Humanité*, and two representatives of the ICRC, Jacques Beaumont and Dominique De Ziegler, who are very kind and considerate towards me. One morning, they invite Jean-Jacques and me to a breakfast *à la française* with croissants, butter, jam and hot chocolate at their hotel. It's impossible to describe how happy we are – since we were set free, our morning meal has consisted of rice and fish. When they receive supplies, they give us bars of milk chocolate with hazelnuts – manna from heaven – tins of stew and sardines in tomato sauce … These products are still unobtainable on the Cambodian market, because as there is still no local currency commerce hasn't been reinstated. At this point we're still being supplied by the Vietnamese with basic goods. The only large international hotel to have reopened makes foreigners pay for their stay in dollars.

Despite these treats, the desire to leave the country still gnaws away at me. After talking with some Cambodians, I even think about getting out through Thailand. But I'm not sure that this is a good idea, and when I talk this project over with my friends from the ICRC, they advise me strongly against it as the roads to Thailand are littered with mines and I discover that they have already killed or wounded many Cambodians. Jacques and Dominique recommend firmly that I wait until I can leave by the normal route.

As a result of telling my story to all the journalists who pass through Phnom Penh, people start to talk about me a bit in France and a short article is published in an issue of *VSD*.[5] One Saturday morning, my sister-in-law Maryvonne, wife of my elder brother Henri, is looking for something to read over the weekend and picks up *VSD* by chance. She later tells me that she never buys that magazine. It's thanks to this article that Henri finds me. It's the hand of destiny that guides him. One morning, I receive a telegram from Henri.[6] It's another emotional shock; I cry all the tears I have stored up in my body. Henri is prepared to send me money for our trip, but I still have to get a visa to leave Cambodia and Vietnam, and it doesn't seem that easy to me.[7] Then I decide to ask the Minister of Health, my boss, for permission to visit my 'family-in-law' in Ho Chi Minh City.

I put in the request at the beginning of November 1979 and, strangely, I get authorisation to leave Phnom Penh straight away. For nine months I've been being assured that no one could do anything for me since France does not have diplomatic representation in the capital – the Khmer and Vietnamese authorities have been tossing my case backwards and forwards between them for months. The Vietnamese, who without doubt blocked my departure until now, must

---

5. *VSD* stands for Vendredi, Samedi, Dimanche (Friday, Saturday, Sunday) and is a popular weekend news magazine.
6. This was another sign of re-birth: the post and telecommunications services were beginning to work again.
7. There was still no air link between Cambodia and France so you had to go through Vietnam.

have thought that the story of a family visit was all the pretext that was needed, although they knew very well from
the very beginning that I had no relatives in Cambodia and
none whatsoever in Vietnam. At this point, I didn't know
that my mother was still alive and that she had ended up in
Tay Ninh – a Vietnamese province close to the Cambodian
border. When I arrived in Ho Chi Minh City, I didn't know
that she was still there and so I left the country without ever
seeing her again.

A week before I leave, I tell my ICRC friends Dominique
and Jacques where I'm really heading. They then give me one
hundred and twenty dollars in small notes and Dominique
encloses a letter of introduction for me to his parents in
case I ever need work. His father is the Swiss ambassador in
Paris; finally he hands me a Metro ticket, telling me: "Here,
Denise, the first time you take the Metro, you'll think of
me." I don't know yet what the Metro is but I store the ticket
away carefully.

At last, the Minister of Health signs my permission: "I
hope this isn't an alibi so that you can leave permanently and
that you'll return in ten days as arranged, right?" I promise
him I will. But he's not fooled. Instead of letting me take
the plane between Phnom Penh to Ho Chi Minh City as I'd
planned, he suggests I keep the *dongs*[8] that the ministry have
given me for my trip and leave in an official convoy that's
going up to the Vietnamese border to distribute medicine to
the Khmer refugees in villages there.

We leave on 10 November 1979. Our luggage consists
of just two *sampots* and two shirts for me and two pairs of
shorts and two shirts for Jean-Jacques – our work clothes.

8. The *dong* is the Vietnamese currency.

For shoes, we only have a pair of rubber flip-flops each, so in order not wear them out, we make the trip barefoot. But it doesn't matter. It's a beautiful day and I'm so happy to weigh anchor from here … The journey takes twenty-four hours because the road between Phnom Penh to the Vietnamese border is in such a bad state. We have to sleep under the stars, but in a totally different atmosphere this time; we're free and our stomachs are nicely full. On the morning of 11 November, after a good breakfast, the convoy sets off again and around nine o'clock in the morning we arrive at the Vietnamese border.

Jean-Jacques and I bid farewell to the Cambodian doctors in the convoy and leave Khmer territory forever, while the convoy carries on its journey along of the border to visit the remote Cambodian villages in the province of Svay Rieng. Bizarrely, we don't encounter a single customs officer or control post, and after we've gone fifty metres or so we find ourselves, without an entry visa, in our first Vietnamese village. I find out how far it is to Ho Chi Minh City and which direction it is. A friendly village woman tells me it's not very far and advises me to go there by bicycle rickshaw. The weather is magnificent, the sky is blue and there's a light, fresh breeze blowing from the north. It's the best time of year. The minister was right; the *dongs* are proving very useful. I hail a rickshaw and show the driver the address of my friend Cécile. To be on the safe side, knowing how things work in the country, I negotiate the price of the ride first. So there we are, the two of us setting off on our new life … I am more relieved every time we get closer to our goal, but Jean-Jacques is always silent. He seems uneasy; he doesn't know my brothers and sister at all but asks no questions and is content to follow me. He talks little and confides even less. I am too preoccupied by our future and don't even think of questioning him, or don't know how to …

It must be about midday when our driver drops us off at the address I've shown him … By chance, it's lunchtime and my friend is home. What a surprise for her, to see us here! Joyfully, but also pulling a face in disgust as we are dirty and barefoot, she shows us the bathroom straight away and lends me trousers and a shirt and Jean-Jacques some shorts and a short-sleeved shirt belonging to her husband. Once we are refreshed and ready, she gives us a snack and asks us to tell her about out trip. Apparently, she was aware that we'd left and was waiting for us to come by plane and not by road. When we're well-rested and well-fed, she suggests that she takes us directly to the French Consul General.

The consulate is guarded like a bunker – *bô-dôi* on every side. It's virtually impossible for a single Asian head to slip through without accreditation. My friend drives through the iron gates with us in the back seat of the car, well hidden, because although I may be French, with my *nhac* features I'm hardly blonde with blue eyes! I am immediately received by the Consul General, François Bouchet, who proves to be very courteous and relieved to see that we've arrived safe and sound. He puts Jean-Jacques and I in the guest house – it's air-conditioned, with all mod cons. This sudden luxury after so many years in the mud starts me crying again, but these are tears of joy and relief as we are finally reintegrating into normal life. Jean-Jacques is silent as ever, and I wonder if he is as reassured as I am. I sense that he's uneasy; he's leaving the country of his childhood for an unknown world, where he'll find a family he'll be meeting for the first time.

Even I, apart from my big sister who came back to Phnom Penh when I was nine, only know my two brothers by an exchange of letters. Yes, it's a big leap into the unknown for me too, but I am too happy to be alive, with my son, safe, away from the hell of the Khmer Rouge ... The consul puts his Vietnamese chef at my disposition: "You only have to order what you feel like eating, please don't hesitate, and I also have a very good wine cellar, ask him for all the bottles you want ..." But I don't take this opportunity, because I'm not at all knowledgeable about wine and with good reason – I have never drunk any! For two days, the chef spoils us with the best Vietnamese dishes and Cécile joins us for these feasts. I will never forget the sensation of rediscovering the pleasure of tasting such good food! Cécile gets along with Jean-Jacques like a house on fire. She lends him a little tape recorder with a Mort Shuman cassette and we play *It's Snowing on Lake Major* continually. During this brief visit to the consulate, I leave the diplomatic compound twice to complete the administrative formalities with the Vietnamese authorities and have neither the opportunity nor the wish to visit Ho Chi Minh City, which I don't know at all.

The morning after our arrival, the vice-consul takes care of our passports. We don't have any identity papers apart from the pass given in Phnom Penh – no photos either, and it's out of the question that we leave the diplomatic compound to go and get some. The vice-consul has the idea of taking a Polaroid of us. The photos are a success and in less than an hour we have proper passports. But I still have to go to the Vietnamese Department of Foreign Affairs to ask for a Vietnamese exit visa. For this, I obviously need to leave the consulate ... Everyone seems a bit anxious as, with my Asiatic features and my *sampot*, there are fears that I'll have difficulty getting past the soldiers on duty. After a long consultation, the vice-consul's wife suggests she lend me a skirt, a shirt and a pair of shoes. Fate is on my side; we are about the same size. Suddenly I am transformed into a real European woman!

The next day, the consul accompanies me to the Vietnamese authorities. I can feel that he's uneasy. At the Department for Foreign Affairs, I'm received alone. He doesn't speak (or doesn't want to speak) a word of French, and makes me tell my whole story in Vietnamese. Then he dissects my passport and the Cambodian *laissez-passer*. He frowns. "How did you get here? There is no entry visa on your *laissez-passer*!" Sweating profusely, I explain how and with whom I left Phnom Penh, and then my journey to Ho Chi Minh City. Total silence. After a few minutes that feel like an eternity, I am entitled to a laconic: "Well, we'll examine the case, you'll have to wait." I meet the consul who is waiting for me in the hall. He asks, still worried, if the lack of an entry visa will cause problems.

Back at the consulate, he invites us to lunch with him. It's totally delicious, a real French meal! Jean-Jacques and I go back to the guest house for a siesta. At three o'clock, the consul returns to his desk, where a call from the Vietnamese Department of Foreign Affairs informs him that my exit visa has been granted! He can't get over it; the usual delay is three weeks to a month, if not more. I'm undoubtedly benefiting from favourable treatment. For nearly nine months, I've moved heaven and earth to leave, and every time I've heard the same answers: "Your country is not represented in Cambodia, we can do nothing", or "Ask your country to intervene in Hanoi". But the situation is resolved! It's astonishing, but I don't try to understand. All that matters to me is that I'm free for good.

So now I can take the first plane leaving for France. All the same (and this is the last recommendation of the Vietnamese authorities to the consul), it would be best, diplomatically if I pay a visit to the head of the diplomatic mission of the Hun Sen government in Ho Chi Minh City to inform him of my departure, given that officially I'm on the staff of the Ministry of Health. The Vietnamese are right, one must be diplomatic. The meeting has actually already been arranged – all I have to do is go there with the consulate's chauffeur. The interview with the head goes well; he asks me to tell him briefly about what I've been through, he is sympathetic and wishes me good luck for the future. That evening, to celebrate our departure, the Consul General takes me, my son, Cécile and her husband to the French Club for a barbeque. What joy to find all these good things after so many years of deprivation … I feel like I'm on cloud nine. The nightmare is truly over and these three days in Ho Chi Minh City really seem like paradise.

To this day, the only regret that haunts me is that not once during this brief stay in Vietnam did the thought of looking for my mother ever cross my mind. People who knew and saw her told me that in 1975, during the first days of the exodus, she left Phnom Penh by the south-west in the direction of the Vietnamese border and ended up in Tay Ninh, a province bordering Cambodia. But I had no idea; I thought that she too had been thrown into the Khmer Rouge's hell and that finding her would be impossible. Later, in Paris, I was distressed to discover that she had died of a heart attack a month after I had passed through Vietnam in December 1979. While leaving the Khmer-Vietnamese border by rickshaw, I passed just by her without knowing ... Why is life so cruel? I will curse myself to the end of my days for not having done anything to find her. I can't deny that at that moment I was obsessed with my own fate. I only had one fixed idea – to leave, fast, and escape from this hell. To save myself, flee, take off ...

13/ Flight

We are scarcely equipped for this great voyage into our new life. Cécile gives me a Samsonite suitcase and some toiletries, while the consul asks her to find us some warm clothes, as we are going to arrive in France right in the middle of November. She buys me a hand-knitted jacket at the Catina street market, which I've still got as a souvenir. Jean-Jacques inherits a pullover and some clothes belonging to my friend's husband, as well as a little calculator, with a watch and musical alarm clock, that makes him happy. I don't possess anything else besides our plane tickets, a few dollars and the Metro ticket given to me by my benefactors at the ICRC. I hide this money carefully in the hem of the trousers I'm wearing, as apparently the highly meticulous Vietnamese customs officers search all travellers from head to foot and take anything of value.

On 15 November 1979, D–Day arrives. The consul and the director of Air France in Ho Chi Minh City accompany us to the airport. A lot of Vietnamese are leaving for Paris and, while queuing, I witness with my own eyes the excessive zeal of the customs officers, who search every passenger, empty the contents of their suitcases, finger and weigh up every object. I panic momentarily, thinking of my trouser hemline. As we approach the ticket booth, I don't feel very reassured. The consul takes my plane tickets and holds them out to the officer in the booth, along with our passports which a customs officer examines for a long time. There's a heavy silence. Several minutes pass that feel like a century. It's as if the world has stopped turning. Then, with two big clunks of the stamp, the official stares at me and Jean-Jacques and indicates, with a courteous smile, that we should pass. He doesn't even look at the suitcase that the consul slides softly along the table. What a surprise! But what a relief as well!

I thank my companions warmly for their kindness and priceless assistance. Here we are in the transit zone between two worlds ... I only know France from books, and the history and geography teachers who made me repeat so many times: "Our ancestors the Gauls!" As I said at the beginning, I am a pure product of colonialism.

Boarding the Boeing 747 that will carry us to our new destiny, I suddenly realise that I'm leaving this part of the world forever. I'm leaving the place I've lived for thirty-five years of my life, full of bitter-sweet memories, for the complete unknown. I'm suddenly overcome by contradictory feelings – nostalgia, relief, serenity too, as we are safe and as free as the air – but also anguish and uncertainty. I don't share my fears with Jean-Jacques but I'm apprehensive about what awaits us; for four years, I have been cut off from everything. How will I manage to fit into a society that I have yet to discover? Before leaving Phnom Penh a member of the *Secours Populaire* delegation asked me: "What will you do in France, Denise? There are a million people unemployed there at the moment. If I were in your shoes, I'd stay in Cambodia; there is so much to do here." Of course, I also have a lot to do, but never again here where I have lived through so many painful things … I tell myself that I still have enough physical and moral strength to move forward. After I've fought so hard to survive, finding work does not frighten me. I'll do hours of cleaning or sweep the streets if I need to! I only pray to the Good Lord while the plane takes off to give me the health I'll need to continue the fight.

Throughout the flight, we are treated like princes. I start chatting to an Australian passenger, who knows my story. He offers me a glass of champagne to celebrate the discovery of my country. Jean-Jacques, always silent, is content simply to watch. He seems happy and at ease and eats all the good things we are served with enthusiasm. The air hostesses give us some souvenirs and Jean-Jacques some games to pass the time.

At Bangkok, I interpret for the air stewardess and tell the Vietnamese who don't understand French that the stop-over will last an hour but that they won't be able to get off. Only Europeans and passengers of other nationalities are author-ised to do so. My son and I take advantage of this break to do some shopping with the precious ICRC dollars that I took out of my hemline after take–off.

We stop for a second time at Abu Dhabi. I don't know why, but the sound of this name, just like that of Dubai, reminds me of daydreams I used to conjure up in my poor and orphaned childhood. This time we don't leave the plane. I look out through the window and am impressed by the stretch of sand we see in the distance. It's the first time I've seen the desert and the first time that I've set eyes on Arabs, who are getting into the plane all dressed in white with their heads covered. I'm discovering a whole new world.

On 16 November 1979, at 11 o'clock in the morning, the plane lands at Roissy-Charles de Gaulle. The pilot announces: "The temperature outside is two degrees, and it's snowing". It's odd, when we arrive, there are no customs controls or police. We pass through like a letter in the post. And, what a fantastic surprise, all the family, alerted by the Quai d'Orsay (the French Foreign Ministry) are here to welcome us, bearing enormous coats: my elder brother Henri, with his five boys, my brother Bernard, and my sister Lydie with her husband Gilbert. I come face to face with my foreign family, with the exception of Lydie, for the very first time. We will have to get to know them. All of them seem adorable, very welcoming and ready to help and to support us. I step onto the French soil, asking myself what is awaiting us, but I also think that it can't be worse than anything that we have lived through before. I'm on cloud nine and can't believe that I have achieved my dream; I've left Cambodia.

The snow falls heavily on the road that leads us to my brother's house in Plaisir. It's the first time Jean-Jacques and I have seen snow. The day after we arrive at Henri's, light snowflakes carry on falling. Jean-Jacques goes out into the garden in his pyjamas, barefoot, and opens his mouth wide to taste the white snowflakes, under the amused watch of his five flabbergasted cousins …

I also remember standing in front of the family dog's food bowl in amazement. One morning, a few days after our arrival, I watched my sister-in-law prepare a saucepan of rice with carrots, leeks and large chunks of beef, assuming this meal was meant for the family. When I discovered that the bourguignon was for the dog, I almost fell over backwards. In Cambodia, even in normal circumstances, the dogs were fed with the leftovers … My astonishment and shock provokes hilarity all round and in my sister-in-law in particular!

After a week, I am called to the office of the Minister for Foreign Affairs. Received by a technical advisor, I recount the drama I've lived through and of my encounter with the Vietnamese. I want the whole world to be aware of the horrors that took place in Cambodia and the general public to understand that if it hadn't been for the Vietnamese intervention, all Cambodians would have been eliminated. The advisor chooses to overlook the subject and lets me know gently that, for the moment, I must no longer focus on these matters and that it would be better if I try to forget, take care of my health and find a job. The department will help me settle in the heart of the 'big house'. I'm very touched by all this attention, but I don't understand why I can't praise my Vietnamese rescuers. Today, with hindsight, rereading press cuttings from this period, I understand how these issues were dividing the international community. At the time, I just wanted to get on with my life …

While I wait to find work, I keep myself busy by going around with a nun I met in Phnom Penh, Sister Françoise Vandermersch, who is responsible for the association and journal *Echange*, which deals with Vietnam, Laos and Cambodia and organises meetings to tell French people about what went on in the Cambodian paddy fields. One day in December, she takes me to Guéméné-Penfao, a small village near Nantes. It's my job to talk about what I have been through, and explain how I got out with the help of the Vietnamese. At the end of the evening, a priest in a cassock with blue eyes approaches me and murmurs in perfect Cambodian: "My child, I advise you to not repeat what you have just said tonight. Be very careful in future, otherwise … you could have problems." Then he disappears. Panicked, and despite Françoise's reassuring words, I decide to not help her in her mission any longer.

The attitude of the official at the Ministry of Foreign Affairs and the warning from that mysterious priest deeply disturbs me; the terrifying atmosphere created by the regime that I have just undergone will do the rest. I'll be quiet, at least in public, for more than twenty-five years … until today.

Two weeks after our arrival, Henri enrols Jean-Jacques at the Plaisir secondary school. At fifteen, he should be in Year 10. But he is forced to start again, with an exemption, in Year 7. At home his cousins will help him a lot and in the next school year he will be able to follow the Year 8 syllabus despite being four years behind. He will need to work twice as hard though.

Other more material worries now await me. I still don't have any work and to benefit from medical insurance for us both, I must enrol in a hostel that welcomes French people from abroad and I can't take Jean-Jacques. So, I leave him at Plaisir with my elder brother Henri. A new separation – this time temporary. Jean-Jacques isn't very comfortable with this but I explain why I have to do this, assuring him that I'll come back every weekend. I know his five cousins will take good care of him.

Here I am, once more embarked upon a new journey. The committee which deals with the repatriation of French people from abroad directs me to the Sarcelles transit centre for the first night, until they find me a room in a hostel in the Paris region. I can still see myself that foggy December evening, being greeted icily reception by the women in charge, who look me up and down and give me a coat and a pair of shoes, asking abruptly: "Size?" But having come from a country where clothes and shoes are made to measure, I'm unable to give all these details to my new compatriots. Result: they unload anything that they can lay their hands on on me. A little later, after a frugal and lonely dinner in the hostel canteen, I wander sadly around the deserted streets of Sarcelles, on my own, in a too-big, too-long brown woollen dressing gown that is masquerading as a coat and on my feet a pair of size forty shoes ... I look like a homeless person who has been dressed in hurry ...

The following day, I'm transferred to the hostel of Montigny-lès-Cormeilles, in the Val-d'Oise, where I'll stay three weeks. I'm allocated a bedroom with a sink, a bed, a table and a chair. The toilets, the showers and the kitchen are communal. With the thirty francs allotted to me per day, I feed myself on bread, camembert and bananas ... The situation is drearier than ever but I must pass this test in order to qualify for medical assistance and to get help finding a job. In any case, it's a thousand times better than my hut in Loti-Batran. And Henri does not abandon me. On Friday evening, he comes to get me to spend the weekend with Jean-Jacques and the rest of the family.

I must admit that despite my gratitude towards France, my country of asylum, my morale is at its lowest. But I don't stop fighting, even if the idyllic universe that I always dreamed of, and that so many people in the Third World still dream about, is a fantasy. You must always work hard, fight every day to not go under, to be accepted and to fit in. Fight? From 1975, this is all I have done, a little bit less or a little bit more ...

I also can't and do not want to stay idle for too long. A week after my arrival in the hostel, to the great displeasure of the head of the centre who does not understand my hurry, I begin to look for work. I decide to contact my last employer in Phnom Penh, the department of Cultural Relations in the Ministry of Foreign Affairs, even if I was only recruited in 1974 as a local. It doesn't take long to get a response – one that's completely discouraging. The Director General advises me in a very paternalistic manner that, despite my diplomas and references, he can only suggest that I take the category A or B *concours* in the ministry. For anyone who's grown up in France, the word *concours* has a specific meaning, but for someone there for the first time, fresh out of the forest, it is not at all obvious. I learn subsequently that to pass a *concours* or examination, you must do specific training beforehand, which for me basically means to start studying again. But in my situation the priority is to find work, because I haven't a centime to live on.

This response leaves me in despair; I marshal my courage and write to the president, Valéry Giscard d'Estaing, to explain my situation to him. He replies to my letter promptly, telling me that he has asked the Ministry for Foreign Affairs to re-examine my case. I can still see my brother's astounded face when he opened the door to the gendarme who brought me the letter from the Élysée, the official residence of the French President, as I hadn't told him what I had done. Thanks to this valuable intervention, I manage to emerge from the abyss. Michel Deverge, my old head at the French embassy in Phnom Penh, for whom I had worked for only a few months, gave me a gift of one thousand francs, an enormous sum at the time, as soon as he heard of my return from hell. He immediately told all his friends about me, who also sent gifts. All this help was extremely precious and allowed me to keep my head above water.

A few weeks later, I'm called to see the personnel department at the Ministry of Foreign Affairs where, after passing a typing exam, I'm offered a short-term contract as a typist. I don't turn up my nose at it – I'm just so happy to have found work. But things still aren't that secure, as the person in charge of the personnel department, irritated by my approach to the Élysée, reminds me at every opportunity that my contract is not likely to be renewed as they're expecting the arrival of a number of graduates from the next *concours*.

Desperate to hold on to this precious job, I decide to learn shorthand. Here, once again, it turns out to be a real assault course. The ministry does in fact give lessons, but only to people who've already acquired the basics, which I have not. On a salary of seven hundred francs I can't pay for a complete training course at the Pigier school, which costs three thousand five hundred francs. So, I go to the bookshop Gibert Jeune, where I buy a second-hand book on Prévost-Delaunay method. From then on, I start studying without a break, every evening till midnight or one in the morning and every weekend, working on the floor, with empty cardboard boxes for a desk, because the council flat in Val d'Argenteuil that I have just been given is still three quarters empty. The hostel generously gave us two small iron beds, two mattresses, white sheets, two bedcovers and two pillows as well as two glasses, two plates, two sets of cutlery, a saucepan, a stove, a bowl, a plastic bucket, a short-handled brush, a dustpan and a gas range. It's real luxury! I live like this for a year, economising centime by centime, before being able to equip myself more. My only treat is a little radio cassette player for my shorthand exercises. For my wardrobe, I accept the clothes offered by friends of the family, without worrying too much about my appearance.

After six relentless months of work, I finally master the method. Now, all I need is to get my speed up. To do this, I apply for a training course at the ministry. But the person in charge looks me up and down derisively when I admit to him that I have only just learnt the basics. I can still hear his caustic response: "Do you know that lessons are reserved for students who have at least sixty to seventy words a minute? How will you keep up if you have no speed? You'll hold everyone back!" I don't let him put me down and beg him to accept my application, promising I'll do everything not to disturb the lesson. He's not convinced but still gives me a chance. The first lessons are very hard to follow. Luckily, the teacher turns out to be kind and understanding. She offers to lend me dictation cassettes that I listen to again and again every evening, all the while trying to get the stuff down in shorthand.

After six months of intensive work, I can at last enrol myself on the first shorthand-typing *concours*. First attempt, first failure. Then, the third time, a year and a half later, I finally pass the famous *concours* and get a permanent job. I'm very proud but above all very relieved. Familiarising myself bit by bit with the cogs of the ministry, I end up understanding what a *concours* is and from then on will never stop competing to better my situation. With my C grade salary I can live adequately, but to improve our daily lot and give Jean-Jacques a bit more, I don't hesitate to take on extra typewriting work at home every night, and to be on duty on Saturday mornings at the Quai d'Orsay. This goes on for ten years.

If at a glance this daily life seems difficult, it's nothing compared to the hell that I have lived through. And we have now also found a family which gives us a lot of moral support. My brother Henri helps Jean-Jacques enormously in his studies and, in the end, adopts, mindful of the father he lost so young. A few years later, in April 1986, unhappily, we suffer another terrible emotional shock when Henri is struck down by a heart attack one night having dinner with friends. While Jean-Jacques almost strangles the emergency paramedic, not understanding that he is incapable of saving his uncle. This new treatment devastates him for a long time and he becomes more secretive with his emotions than ever …

He continues, however, to slave away at school without complaining, helped by his cousins and a few charitable teachers living nearby. He succeeds, little by little, in catching up with what he has missed and joins the right school year. Fighting against all the odds, just as he fought in the camps, he has managed today to make himself a little place in the sun.

And by November 1979 I am able to see my son, a mature boy of fifteen, pick up a normal school and social life just like other young people his age, happy to find work again, a family, health and strength, happy to be free – just happy ... And I will always be grateful to France for having welcomed us and offered us a better life.

I left the Third World, with its endless stream of unhappiness and misery. But I also left the most beautiful years of my life there – to put myself back together in a society of quite another dimension, an unforgiving society advancing at a hundred miles an hour, where you must defend yourself every day, struggle constantly and take up challenges at every instant just to survive.

Another kind of fight...

Conclusion

I've now been at home in France for twenty-five years.

I turned the page and began a new life, but I've had to fight to fit in. The civil service has offered me a second chance. After ten years in the central administration of the Ministry of Foreign Affairs, I found a job as bilingual secretary at the Institute for Security Studies, today an agency of the European Union. So, as well as being French, I now feel that a part of me is European.

I met Robert, a Swiss German living in Paris and we were married in 1994. He adopted my family, Jean-Jacques and his daughter Aurélie Phou, on whom I lavish all the love I couldn't give my poor Jeannie.

In this book, I wanted to bear witness to the monstrous regime of the Khmer Rouge and pay homage to my liberators, the soldiers of the regular Vietnamese army, who waged a war against the most bloodthirsty ideology of our time, the Maoist communism that inspired Pol Pot.

Unfortunately, the cries, whether they are of hate or mourning, don't bring back the dead. I only pray that their souls rest in peace. They are always with me, buried at the bottom of my heart with the memories I do not want to disturb.

DONATION

Part of the profits from the sale of *To the End of Hell* will be given to the Documentation Center of Cambodia (DC-Cam), where a scholarship has been set up in the name of Denise Affonço's nine-year old daughter, Jeannie, who starved to death under the Khmer Rouge regime.

DC-Cam is an independent research institute that provides a crucial source of information about this tragic period in Cambodian history for academics, lawyers, activists and the general public.

DC-Cam has two main objectives. Firstly, to record and preserve the history of the Khmer Rouge regime for future generations. Secondly, to compile and organise information that can serve as potential evidence in any forthcoming trials of members of the Khmer Rouge. It believes that memory and justice are the foundations for the rule of law and genuine national reconciliation in Cambodia.

The Center was originally set up by the Cambodian Genocide Programme at Yale University as a field office. It became an independent Cambodian research institute in 1997. Find out more at: www.dccam.org

To make a donation, please send a cheque to:
The Documentation Center of Cambodia,
66c, Preah Sihanouk Blvd, P.O. Box 1110,
Phnom Penh, Cambodia
Tel: 00 (855) 23 211-875.
Or contact: Sophorn Huy
email: sophornhuy@yahoo.com

Please include a covering letter quoting the reference: Jeannie